A Celtic Book of Dying

"Phyllida draws from the deep wellsprings of the ancient spiritual and ancestral memory of Ireland. Our ancestral memory concerning life and death that embodies connections with the natural world and its rhythms. Life understood as a river of presence that flowed in and out of many different forms, and death was understood as a natural part of the continuum of life, death, and rebirth. Earlier cultures saw death as a transformation of form rather than the end of life. These insights are urgently needed in our death-phobic culture. This book is a wonderful spiritual, philosophical, and practical resource to educate and guide people who are dying and those who are journeying with them. With insights, practices, prayers, and blessings to support the journey for everyone involved, this book offers all of us an amazing opportunity to grow in awareness, in consciousness, and in unconditional love and acceptance."

—**Dolores T. Whelan**, M.Sc. Biochemistry, guide, healer, and teacher
within the Celtic spiritual tradition and author of
Ever Ancient Ever New: Celtic Spirituality in the Twenty-First Century

"Phyllida writes with a natural flowing style that invites the reader in. *A Celtic Book of Dying* is a gift for those wishing to know more about the dying process and an invaluable aid in assisting a dying loved one. I highly recommend it."

—**Barbara Vincent**, M.A., RGN, RHV, RNT, priestess of Brigid

"When Phyllida Anam-Áire speaks, writes, or sings, she takes you on a soul's journey! *A Celtic Book of Dying* will take you to a deeper understanding of Celtic consciousness that encompasses conscious dying as well as conscious living, as the one cannot be understood without the other. Everything Phyllida teaches comes out of her own experience and is therefore always authentic. I am deeply grateful for the wisdom she is passing on to us and for encouraging us always to embody this wisdom and to live it instead of understanding it intellectually."

—**Le Grá Mór, Jolanda Aoisanam Marks**, psychologist
and initiate of Brigid

"This sacred book contains an extremely precious sharing of a deeply rooted knowledge and wisdom, focussing on both the biological as well as the spiritual process of dying. It offers us an opportunity to approach death with open hearts and with less fear, so we can be more present for our own death, for being a witness or sitting with another who is dying, and in supporting those whose loved ones are dying. Working with Phyllida you find yourself in a powerful cauldron in which to face all aspects of yourself, including those that may have previously been cut off or denied, so that you can welcome all of yourself home, sit in the fullness of you, and live the whole of who you are. Life becomes an amazing and vibrant journey of preparation for death."

—**Bryony Smith**, M.Sc., biodynamic cranial therapist

"Although this book is entitled *A Celtic Book of Dying,* it is very much about the living and how to live. Phyllida is our loving and empowering guide upon *The Path of Love in the Time of Transition,* as the subtitle says. Deep insights are communicated with honesty, passion, and practicality. Poetry, song, stories, and rituals are interwoven in a comforting and reassuring way. It is written with great compassion and has an authority that is always rooted in true experience. I don't believe that one could read a book like this and not be changed by it. I know these teachings helped me to accompany my father in the dying process, because they freed me to truly listen to myself and to him, and, as a result, I have a beautiful memory of the gift of his passing. I also know that there is enough teaching in this book to keep my heart and soul inspired for the rest of my life."

—**Cecilia Rose Kane,** teacher (retired), writer, and storyteller

A CELTIC BOOK OF DYING

The Path of Love
in the Time of Transition

PHYLLIDA ANAM-ÁIRE

FINDHORN PRESS

Findhorn Press
One Park Street
Rochester, Vermont 05767
www.findhornpress.com

Text stock is SFI certified

Findhorn Press is a division of Inner Traditions International

Originally published in 2005 under the title:
A Celtic Book of Dying: Watching with the Dying, Travelling with the Dead
Revised and updated edition published in 2022. Both editions by Findhorn Press

Disclaimer
The information in this book is given in good faith and intended for information
only. Neither author nor publisher can be held liable by any person for any loss
or damage whatsoever which may arise from the use of this book or any of the
information therein.

Cataloging-in-Publication data for this title is available from the Library of
Congress

ISBN 978-1-64411-298-4 (print)
ISBN 978-1-64411-299-1 (ebook)

Printed and bound in the United States by Lake Book Manufacturing, Inc.
The text stock is SFI certified. The Sustainable Forestry Initiative® program
promotes sustainable forest management.

10 9 8 7 6 5 4 3 2 1

Edited by Michael Hawkins
Text design and layout by Richard Crookes
This book was typeset in Adobe Garamond Pro

To send correspondence to the author of this book, mail a first-class letter to the
author c/o Inner Traditions • Bear & Company, One Park Street, Rochester, VT
05767, USA, and we will forward the communication, or contact the author
directly at **seabheann@icloud.com**.

This book is dedicated
to Dr Elisabeth Kübler-Ross
and to Brigid of Ireland.

Elisabeth guided me on the path I was to walk
since our first meeting in 1982, and has been
accompanying me with Brigid of Ireland.

Brigid on the other hand
has been in me
since birth.

Contents

PART FOUR
BEING WITH THE BEREAVED

PART FIVE
LESSONS FROM THE HEART OF NATURE

PART SIX
STORIES FROM THE HEART OF DEATH

APPENDIX

Glossary of Gaelic Words and Expressions

Ag dul amach, ag dul isteach [Egg dull amack, egg dull is chaa]: *Going out, going in*

Áit an dorchas mór [Atch an dorkass more]: *Place or passage of great darkness*

Áite [Atcha]: *Place or passage*

An Corda geal [An korda gal]: *The bright, or silver, cord*

An Earrach [An Yarrack]: *Spring*

An Fomhair [An four]: *Autumn*

An Geimhreadh [An Give-rew]: *Winter*

An Samhraidh [An Sow-ruh]: *Summer*

An Tursach mór [An Tursach more]: *The great tiredness*

Anam-Áire [Anam aye-rah]: *Soul carer*

Anam-Cara [Anam kara]: *Soul friend*

AnamA-le-Céile [Anama le kayla]: *Souls together*

Cain [Ka-yn]: *Energetic nervous system*

Ceile De [Kaz-la jay]: *Together with God*

Croí oscailte [Kree us kailte]: *Open heart*

Filid [Fillid]: *Poets*

Fios [Fis]: *Wisdom*

Glóire an Anam [Gloy-re an Anam]: *Glory of the soul*

Guth an Anam [Gooh an Anam]: *Voice of the soul*

Lán do Grásta [Lan doh Grasta]: *Full of Grace*

Meitheal [Mehall]: *Gathering*

Samhain [Sow-ayn]: *Halloween*

Scéalta [Skealta]: *Stories*

Seá [Sha]: *As in "ho" or "amen", "yes"*

Seábhean [Sha-van]: *Female shaman, saying yes to life, or old wise woman*

Solasú [Sol-assu]: *Light-bringer*

Tír-na-nÓg [Cheer na nog]: *Land of eternal births, Heaven*

Tir-na Sorcha [Cheer na Sorka]: *Land of brightness*

Tobar Beatha [Tuber baha]: *Well of life*

Trasna [Trasna]: *Cross over*

Tuatha de Dannan [Tooha day Dannan]: *Tribe or people of the God Dannan*

"An Mac a bhfuil beannacht a Athair aige, is e solas a dhorcas fein." [An Mack a will Bannacht a Ahar egga, is eh solas a gorkas feign.]: *"The son with the Father's blessing is a light unto himself."*

"Beidh at teacht abhaile a grá." [Bay egg tch-acht awella a gra.]: *"Be coming home, dear one."*

"Is ar scath a chéile a mhaireann na daoine." [Is air skah a kay-la a warren na deena.]: *"It is in the shadow of each other we live."*

"Tá críoch leis." [Tha kri-och lesh.]: *"It is finished."*

Introduction

"Watching with the dying, travelling with the dead" is a term not used very often in our day-to-day language. It was however the language used by the old ones when they referred to consciousness, awareness, and presence. To keep watch is to be mindful, to give our full attention, to enter into a deep relationship with, to be soulfully here and now. When Jesus the Christ was experiencing his sense of loss and loneliness in the garden of Gethsemane, he asked if his three good friends would watch with him. He needed this human watchfulness, this presence.

To travel with the dead is again watchfulness, a moving with the soul to its place of rest. It is about soul tracking soul, one soul journeying with the soul of the other and helping it, if needed, to release further and deeper into itself, into unconditional love. With sensitivity and unobtrusive awareness one's soul may be the *Anam-Áire*—the soul carer of another, to re-heart or remind them of their final resting place in the arms of mercy and bliss. With empathetic caring we can be of assistance to another either in the body or in spirit. People who have had to leave their body as children in order to survive abuse etc., can easily transverse the worlds of creation. As long as they have done their healing work and are able to stay grounded in their bodies now, they can be of great help to souls departing the earth. They work with the energetic fields of awareness and can integrate the darkness into the light.

I first met with the concept of "watching with the dying, travelling with the dead" when I was working with dying patients and their relatives. During my times of deep inspirational meditations, I would enter into an altered state and, during one of these altered states of consciousness I received knowledge which later on structured itself into a series of writings called "Teachings from the Cauldron", also known as "Wisdom from the Cauldron". It felt to me that these teachings were Celtic in origin, as they first were transmitted through the medium of the old Irish language and especially from the energetic field of the great feminine or soul archetype, Brigit.

Since this time I have been taught by the soul alone and for this grace I am deeply grateful.

How I Met with the Teachings

When I was given the "Teachings from the Cauldron on Death and Dying" according to our Celtic Goddess Brigit (later adopted by the Catholic Church in her transmuted status of Saint Brigid), I was living in Findhorn, in the north of Scotland. Having given a presentation and workshop at a Conference titled, Conscious Living, Conscious Dying, in April 1998, I decided to live there for a while.

One Sunday morning I had a great desire to sit down and write prayers in Gaelic. As I did so, tears flowed down my face and my heart expanded in my chest. I did not understand what was happening but I kept on writing poems in the old Irish language, beautiful poems depicting life and death in a way that honoured our courage to incarnate as the "clay stuff of God". An example of conscious dying is expressed in the following:

"Loosen my arms and let me fly

Straight to the throat of God.

And be the bird

That sings a love song to your beauty.

Close down my eyes and let me touch

All of creation with your love

So I can see with only kindness and mercy.

Zip up my ears so I am deaf

And let my inner ear awaken to your breath.

Pour out the old wine from my heart

And fill each empty glass with your compassion.

Distract me wildly with your heart's drumming

And let me fall right off my path and become the way.

Open wide my book of understanding

And tear out every reason why I might love you.

Feed not my soul with wholesome rice

But with sweet honeyed spice

That falls like healing from your eyelids, Beloved."

As I continued writing, I felt an intense sense of beauty and pain, joy and sadness all at the same time. I felt at one with all creation and the deepest grief and most exquisite joy flowed into my veins. I thought my heart would burst open, the feelings were so intense. The splendour, order and beauty of all created phenomena touched my soul and at the same time I could experience the unbelievable grief and suffering of the world. Images of death and life, joy and pain, God and devil, good and bad, old and young, night and day etc., flooded me like I was experiencing all life in the wink of an eye. I could feel my heart beat in everything I touched, in the pen with which I wrote, in the feel of the paper on the table, in the energy around me. Colours danced back at me with vibrant intensity and sounds were magnified as if heard through a loudspeaker.

What was happening to me? I had had a near-death experience in 1973; this felt very much like it. I was not frightened; I knew I was all right. Somehow I felt that someone/thing bigger than me was in charge and was overseeing it all. I later realized that I was experiencing the great merciful heart energy of the Cosmic Mother and Jesus and that the compassion I felt for all living things including myself came from them. I was seeing us all through the eyes of pure love and I could hardly bear it. Death and life were one, letting go and receiving danced together in a sea of delight and I was allowed to share in this miracle and I was humbled.

When I felt in need of comfort I would sit and read one of the poems that flowed from my pen. I seemed to drink from them like a woman might drink from a clear and refreshing pool.

At the same time a Canadian priestess called Saoirse (Gaelic for "freedom") was visiting. She was an academic in Celtic studies and was very interested in my growing encounters with Brigit of the Celts. I mentioned the "Wisdom from the Cauldron". At that stage I did not know what this wisdom was, I only knew that I was somehow tuning into it and Saoirse felt that I should combine psychological principles with a deep feminine spirituality.

I later understood that the Cauldron symbolizes the soul, the *anima*, she who experiences the fullness of life in all its expressions. The magic Cauldron is spoken of a lot in Celtic mythology. It was an alchemical vessel, as was the Grail, and a sacred container for the Feminine, the soul, and the passionate fire of love. Brigit was the great stirrer, bringing to the surface that which needed to be made conscious. Eventually all is stirred back to love.

Seemingly the Cauldron of Brigit was the oracle from whose rich contents the Celts founded their spiritual belief. It portrayed a matriarchal approach in ways of relating to one another in the *meitheal*, or community. Many rituals and ceremonies were celebrated with the use of the sacred Cauldron.

The ancient Irish translation for cauldron, "that which holds all with equal weight", describes it well.

In 1999, I was initiated as a priestess of Brigid and this launched me on my journey with Brigit as my strong inner Goddess archetype and Jesus as my compassionate archetype. Not realizing the significance of the gesture then, I was given the gift of the cauldron by the Newbold House Community in Forres, Scotland. It has been a sacred source of teaching. I was instructed not to read any books referring to Celtic death rites but to follow only the inner teachings and to let others share them through workshops and talks. As the Celts left us a grand oral tradition regarding teachings and beliefs, it seems right that I give you these teachings in the form of stories from the hearth. I firmly believe that when we lose sight of the stories of our ancestors, we lose some vital inner way of seeing.

It is from the innate storyteller in me that I share these stories with you. May they inspire you to tell your stories, too, and to honour your own "my-story" (mystery) of life and death.

My Own Story:
In Grief Did My Mother Conceive Me

In the year 1943, my parents had three children: Mary, aged 4; Eileen, aged 2-and-a-half; and Charles, aged 8 months. My mother was a teacher and my father had a business. They were both renowned for their musical abilities in singing and playing the piano. Father was also an actor in local amateur dramatics and Mother had a great gift for composing songs and sketches. Life was good and they were well-known and well-loved in their village. One day while Mother was bathing Charles, he took convulsions and died in her arms. She tried everything a mother could have done to resuscitate her baby. Father felt totally helpless and distraught. At the graveside, Mother was crying her grief naturally and Father was behind her, supporting her and being strong for her as that was the male role in those days. However, the parish priest thought she had cried enough and, as he approached her, he placed his hand on her shoulder and said; "Now, Mrs McGill, no more tears or God will send you a further cross; it is God's will and we have to accept it."

I can only imagine the pain this caused these two grieving, sad people. God's will was brutal; it took their child. As the last sod of turf was placed on the grave, these two lonely, grieving people walked home with the help and love of their community. Grandmother advised my parents to go to Father's sister for a week and she and Grandfather would care for Mary and Eileen. This they decided to do the next morning. With instructions from the two girls to "be sure and get them furry gloves", my Parents set off on their long journey to Dublin on the Tuesday morning. They decided to come home early as Mother was getting worried about the girls. They began their journey back to Donegal that cold Sunday in February 1943.

"Why is everyone standing outside our house, John?" Mother asked nervously.

"Probably they had not seen us at the funeral and have come to pay respects."

Mother's brother, a priest, took her by the hand and told her the news that their wee child Eileen had died the day after they went to Dublin. Mother stifled a scream and fainted. Father felt totally hopeless and helpless. Neither could show signs of so-called weakness. The agony had to be stifled inside, deep inside, and never ever must it leak out. Imagine their sorrowing as they stood together at the foot of the small cot in which their child lay, snowdrops in her hand, a smile on her face and the golden curls falling on her forehead.

My mother told us later that she wished she could have died with the child. Death, she said, would have been a mercy but she had to remember what the parish priest in his "Godly wisdom" had said about God's will. Thus they held back the howl of pain which longed for expression, the active grieving that could have helped their human hearts to open, to themselves and to each other. From then on the music stopped in our home. From then on, Father drank to help him to cope with the sorrow he felt. From then on Mother spent more and more time alone or praying in the Chapel. From then on the silence between them lengthened. From then on the radio was not turned on. From then on Mary had to be good, had to be quiet and play alone. From then on "God's will" became the motto of our household and no one was allowed to question it at any time or there could be a further cross and this might be . . . Mary.

In May of that year, three months after the burial of their two children, I was conceived. It was time for the woman to "do her duty towards her husband". My mother, still silently grieving, also dreaded becoming pregnant again. I was born nine months later. If we are to believe that the child in the womb experiences the mother's emotions, then I certainly felt her unshed tears and her deep, unspoken, unexpressed fear. I believe I had the best school wherein to learn the lessons about loss and the sorrows and side-effects of inactive grief. I learned all this from the womb of my mother and from having lived with my parents in a house where God's will governed all. Tears of "self-pity" were not allowed.

The greatest relief for me, however, was school holidays with Nanny McDyre. She in her earth wisdom introduced me to another way of being, the way of nature and her healing rituals; together with an unfathomable store of stories and boiled sweets, she fed my impressionable soul, with respect for the mystery and magick (the old, feminine spelling) of things invisible. My rich Irish background, guarded by the mountains and the Atlantic, steeped in the Gaelic language, wrapped up in earth symbology and superstitions, left a deep imprint on my soul as a child, the gifts of which I only realized many years later. I am grateful that my mind is nourished by other food when a world of instant access to information and other so-called technological devices try to seduce me from the still, small voice that informs me from within. The voices of my ancestors sing my bones alive and echo louder in me than the loudest advertisement.

I went to a boarding school run by nuns at twelve years of age, and the insignia of the Louis order, *Dieu le veult*, (God wills it) was not difficult to embrace; it was already indelibly printed on my psyche. Years later, having been a nun and left the convent, I married a Protestant, lived in Northern Ireland for 26 years, birthed two children, grieved the death of good friends, had a near-death experience, many out-of-body experiences, buried both parents, divorced, was without a home, or much money and grieved the death of relationships, worked internationally and in America with Elisabeth Kübler-Ross, M.D., created my own workshops, made three CDs of my own music and songs, wrote my autobiography, a book of poems etc. … I realized more and more the depth of the inheritance of grief I had agreed to when I incarnated and the wealth of resources I had also attracted to facilitate the healing of my life.

In 1983, I met Elisabeth Kübler-Ross and I began the journey of healing my past grief whilst I learnt the tools with which to deal with future grief. It seemed natural for me to work in the field of death and dying and life began to take its natural shape in me. My past had helped me find who I am and for that I am eternally grateful. With my eventual priesting initiation I could feel my soul's homecoming strongly. Ritual and ceremony were no strangers to me; I was a natural *Seábhean* (Gaelic feminine name for "shaman"). My childhood holidays with my Nanny McDyre amongst nature and my rich inheritance of Irish dancing, poetry, singing and a deep attraction for the Gaelic language were all powerful catalysts for my later work. Fifty years later, a Maiden, Mother and Crone, I was ready to sprout my Celtic roots, ready to move into a new life. My new name gave me the power to do so, that of *Anam-Áire*, carer of the soul.

Brigit, Stirrer of the Cauldron

The Celtic Goddess Brigit was the stirrer of the Cauldron of Immortality, that powerful container of birth and death, which held all, in balance and harmony. She was the true archetype of Virgin, Mother and Crone and was the daughter of the great Dagda, the wise and honoured God of the *Tuatha de Dannan*. She was also guardian of the Cauldron of Plenty. I clearly understand Brigit as being the shape-changing, alchemical power of love on earth. Saint Brigid was known for her fiery passionate ways, her outspokenness, her skills as a metalsmith, and her love and caring for the dying. She was poet, storyteller, and wise woman. The flame of Brigit still burns deep in the Celtic soul for we are no strangers to the fires of love's all-purifying embers. Like all gods, goddesses and saints, Brigit is not relegated to time.

Forever she reigns in the underworld kingdoms of the unconscious and from that moist and mysterious bed she sets about shape-changing our psyches. From there she creeps around groaning, sensing, gathering, stirring, all the parts that have been left parched and unattended to in us. She is Kali Shakti; she is destroyer and lover. She is the weeder, the planter, who waters the seeds of our wholesomeness, holiness that got windswept in the storms of our uprooting from grace. She claws at the map of our own landscape and homes our trembling feet when we turn, twist, shake and tumble on our way back. She always shows us the way back; back into, not out of, our own thickets, full of luscious undergrowth and sticky-smelling stuff. She points out the flowers in the compost of our unlived potential and we run for fear of our own beauty. We hate her, yet we honour her nourishing wilderness. We want to strangle her and at the same time mould ourselves to her shadows. Whatever we do, however we try to ignore her, or shake her off, she persists. She never condemns us or abandons us, though at times we plead with her to do so. She knows that her work is to shake our inner, deepest foundations and build us up anew, and stronger than we could ever have imagined. She threatens our stubborn attraction to duality and her ultimate goal is that we *honour our divinity in the fullness of our humanity*.

No matter how long we remain outside her transformational Cauldron, we know that one day we will have to surrender to her call of the wild in us. One day we will have to bow to the truth of our own divinity and on that day we will have started the journey to the centre of ourselves. On that day we will have come home like the prodigal, home to feast and the making of love. On that day we will have surrendered to the voice of our own soul and the marriage of soul and ego will have taken place and we will sing our own hallelujah. And we do not have to wait until we are out of the body to do so.

On that day we will have tasted our own liberation whilst still "in-bodied" (embodied).

The spiritual climate would seem to be right now for the emergence of this mighty transformer and shape-changer amongst us. It is time to bring consciousness into our daily living and our daily dying. The Celtic heart is one that is broken and strengthened daily in its dying to dualism. The Celtic heart is willing to embrace death and life in one breath.

Why do I sense that the work of Brigit is becoming more evident at this time? My immediate answer is, I feel her energy at work in our willingness to look fully in the eyes of the great transformer, death, and be held captive no longer by our own fears of life.

PART ONE

Death and Dying
in the Celtic Tradition

Opening the Heart to Death

> "Can you be with me in the cold morning of dying?
> When the fire in me is out and nothing warms my blood
> Can you watch with the eye of a mother?
> When the candle is burnt and the friends have gone?
> Can you just be, not wishing one more breath in me?
> And when my eyes are closed shut,
> Glad of the long quiet rest
> Will you then travel still with me?
> As I close this door behind
> And open into the open heart of death
> Sweet love call that brought me birth,
> Now calls me safely back in earth."

This poem, originally in Gaelic, came through me when I was in primary school. It is one I have remembered for over half a century, with a sense of wonder in the original language. As a young person I found this poem strangely comforting as it regarded death and dying in a friendly way and asks the carer to "watch with the eye of a mother" and simply "be, not wanting one more breath in me". The "watcher" was asked to "travel still with me" as the dying person was taking a journey "into the open heart of death".

This reference to opening into "the open heart of death" is interesting; it seemed that the old ones saw death as all-inclusive, all-embracing, like an *Anam-Cara* (soul-friend) who gives the "long rest" and sings a "sweet love call" that "calls me safely back in earth".

This idea of a love call calling us to "in-body" and calling us back to spirit again, is part of Celtic belief regarding birth and death. They believed that a note or sound calls us to embody ("in-body") whilst the same sound in a higher octave calls us to disembody. The closing of the door of earth-life is an initiation that the soul experiences as it entered into the various passages in the spirit world. It is the leaving behind, the experience of decathexis (i.e., where memories etc., no longer arouse emotion) from all material form, the great transformation.

The *Anam-Áire*, carer of the soul, the one who journeys with the soul in the afterlife will "travel still" with it as it opens into the "open heart of death."

How can we possibly talk of the open heart of death when it seems that its sole purpose is to take from us what we love and, furthermore, how can we be expected to open to something that seems to have no regard for life?

How can we sit easily with such a heartless one who steals from us the deep connecting bonds of friends and family and who will eventually take our own breath and leave others bereft and mourning too? Surely it would be insanity to consider inviting the antithesis of life itself into our consciousness!

Indeed, would it not lead to all sorts of unnecessary grief and sorrow and eventually bring only depression and emotional breakdown, encouraging the taking of one's life?

Surely opening the heart to death would be to deny life and all its beauty, energy and abundance. All these statements seem very reasonable and very sensible. And somehow as I write them they speak of a great fear, ignorance and defensiveness, as if the essence of life itself was being threatened and we, the custodians of this precious gift, have a duty to protect it from this beast of prey, this thief death. Considering the immensity of the suffering, the challenges, the seeming arrogance and treachery that death often brings, many of us are left feeling overwhelmed and victimized by its power.

This was not the philosophy of our ancestors the Celts. They were always prepared for that inevitable visitor. Death was seen as a great journey, a great adventure into the vastness of our own nature, into the earth of our self. Death was not seen as a thief in the night, as nature had prepared them well in her changing seasons and moods. Death was seen as a natural way of dealing with *An Tursach mór*, the great tiredness, and they were "glad of the long rest at last".

Contemporary religious education concerning death does not make us more conscious, so most of us spend time and energy avoiding this so-called intruder and, by whatever means, try to keep its stiff, icy fingers off what is near and dear to us. We seem to be of the opinion that this will make it easier for us to live our lives fully, without fear of the future. When life asks us to die the smaller deaths, i.e., to let go of someone or something in order to move on in our lives towards fullness, unwillingness to accept change will not facilitate this. Ignoring the inevitability of death will not help us to have a deeper respect for this life and live it more consciously moment by moment.

Closing our eyes to anything creates fear and fear keeps us ignorant of facts and ignorance of the facts keeps us unconscious. We are here in our earth bodies to widen and deepen our consciousness so that we will have eyes that can see and ears that can hear as Jesus the Christ advised. Partial seeing shuts us down, blinds us to a wider more all-encompassing reality that accepts birth and death as the unique ways in which life expresses itself in form and out of form. Consciousness is the opposite of avoidance. The more our awareness widens into our psyches the more we will be able to see through the eyes of unconditional or impersonal love.

In other words, consciousness provides us with a new means of connecting, of communicating, of knowing. It enables us to see and hear the hidden or symbolic messages in all we encounter. In consciously observing the changing seasons of nature and applying these changes to their own lives, the Celts were enabled to live soulfully and die in the same consciousness. Celtic Christians sought to have with them "The mind of Christ"—i.e., where our egos or earth-minds become one with our essential nature, which is Spirit or Life itself. This mindfulness helps us to know more clearly the purpose of our lives in earth-form and we joyfully realize that life is not threatened by the loss of form, as I detail next.

Life Is Not Threatened
by the Loss of Form

It is our ignorance of this fact that has kept us from looking at death in a more wholesome and holy way. The deep disappointment and despair for many of us is the realization that we are not the controllers of life; that life is, and always has been, and it is not dependent on whether we are in earth-form or spirit. What Celtic consciousness has taught me is that our individual soul is subject to the guidance of spirit/life as it is the messenger of spirit which brings the abundance of energy to our natures. It animates and vitalizes form.

It is so deeply comforting really to know that we as human beings, unique and complex expressions of life, birthed from the vast expanse of life force itself, have something glorious in common with all other expressions of life whether they be in body or not, and that is:

We all have a responsible relationship to this mighty energy in which all created phenomena live and move and have their beingness.

It is not a matter of life being in us for a while, rather we are forever in life and subject to its laws and mysteries.

This is a humbling thought and one that helps to open our hearts in the deepest gratitude to life that sustains and nurtures us in earth and in the life after earth. Our greatness is that our essence is life itself. We come from life: we return to life. This is all. We are forever in life and we cannot escape this fact.

Whilst it would be quite naïve of me to think I can ever comprehend what earth-life and spirit-life are all about, I would, however, like you to join me as we ask for guidance from our Celtic wise old ones to look at the subject of spirit-life and see if we can move from a place of either longing for it to come quickly—so that we do not have to deal with our wretched lives—or seeing it as an empty space of darkness and an end to all life. Maybe we can just reach a more informed state regarding our relationship with it. The belief that death will come as a "thief in the night" only makes sense if we believe that we own life. A thief only takes from us what we rightly own. Celtic consciousness believes that we do not own anything—in nature, not our own souls, not the land, or any aspect of creation. The Celtic idea was that we are the custodians of the earth and our own lives in the earth. It is up to us to guard life, not possess it. If we held this belief and truth we would not so readily rape the earth for gold, metals, crystals etc. And we would not kill the wild things for profit or so called sport.

The belief was that we cannot fully understand the majesty of nature but can only live our lives in reverential relationship to it. Our Celtic ancestors lived their simple lives carrying within their hearts and souls a sense of gratitude to life for the graces they daily received and the gifts so richly bestowed by the great Mother/Father Creator. I feel we have lost that sense of wonder and awe, that sense of deep thanksgiving for the blessings we daily receive from life. With our accumulated knowledge of things seen and unseen it seems that we will never be able to comprehend fully the great mysteries of life and death in such confined intellects and psyches because of our limited earth-consciousness.

If death could speak I believe it would say:

"Here I am,

Open heart of death

Forever present in life.

Open to me

By letting go of every breath

So that life can breathe you freely."

In my work with conscious dying, I have been challenged by my Celtic ancestors to see death not as a betrayer of dreams but as one who, in accordance with the storyline of the dying person, simply or not-so-simply carries out their individual life-script. This may be easy to comprehend in the case of someone who has lived a long and good life and is ready to leave that life. It is not so simple when the dying person is a young soldier on the battlefield or a child who dies in its mother's arms. Our finite earth-minds cannot understand how these can be examples of death assisting us in our life agendas, yet from the perspective of the soul and the lessons it has chosen to learn, all is orderly and all has to be stirred back into love eventually. Each "my story" (mystery) is individual and authentic. One might ask how life can allow such atrocities to happen to good people.

As finite, emotionally-attached beings our assessments of the mysteries of life are limited, our capacity to understand things of the spirit leaves us confused and often bewildered. As long as we hold the belief that a God "up there" regulates every aspect of our lives and sends suffering to one person and joy to another, we will forever stay immature in our spirituality. It is time to cast off the ways of childhood and realize that as free-willed, divine human beings we are responsible for the ways in which we have chosen to "work out our salvation". There are no judgements of our experiences; ego structures alone, judge. We dare not criticize another's path to the centre of themselves because we do not know their life-script. The soul in us longs to "stir all back into love" which ultimately is harmony and equilibrium. How long it takes to achieve this end has to do with whether the ego-mind cooperates with the soul from incarnation to incarnation or not. The soul has her own timing and is neutral. It does not evaluate and this is difficult for our earth-minds to comprehend; however, our essential life-source knows the truth.

In Celtic consciousness, our life experiences are seen as journeys towards *Tir-na-nÓg*, *Tir-na-Sorcha* or "Summerlands", known as that place of forever birth, the land of agelessness. The American Indians called it the "great hunting ground". Here all our stories are gathered-in and we ourselves, together with the goddesses, gods and guardians of the upper worlds, access from a place of openness and detachment what our next journey should be. This detachment from emotionalism is simplified when the earth-mind has been integrated into spirit and the human heart has been absorbed into the universal heart of love itself, free from bonds and attachments.

In this book I invite us both to look at the way our ancestors viewed death and see if we cannot be re-educated, re-socialized and *re-ligionized* in the matters of dying and beyond death and hopefully leave a more wholesome legacy to our children.

If I am the author of my life and I chose to live as consciously as I can, surely this affects the way I go from earth to spirit, from so-called life to so-called death. And there are surprises, of course; just like life itself, nothing is written in stone. Branwen, the Welsh goddess who gave the Cauldron of Immortality to Brigit, was said to possess the gifts of prophecy and could discern, by gazing into the Cauldron, when and how a person would die. Perhaps by contemplating how we live our lives we can prophesy how and when we die. Contemporary Celtic goddesses might suggest that we die as we have lived and we are the creators of our own worlds.

lIFe choices

Look at the things which, in your belief, cause suffering in your life and see where you blame life in the form of another human being, or an event.

Contemplate and look deeply at the perceived causes for this suffering. Might some choices you made in your life have contributed to the suffering? Can you take responsibility for your own part in this?

We cannot blame life anymore. We have to take responsibility for how we live our lives in the earth and that is not easy because it means we have to become conscious of choices we make and these choices, according to our Celtic Wise Ones, influence our final earth journey into spirit. If we dare to open our hearts to life, we are challenged into opening them to death also.

But maybe we have time to take some other journeys before death calls on us, before the *croí oscailte* (open heart) of death invites us to another way of being, one no less full and abundant than the life just lived on the earth plane. It is these journeys that prepare us for the last ride and that are pointers as to how open we can be to life in spirit.

We can reach liberation before death; the question is: Are we willing to open our hearts to the abundance of life, here and now? If we are, then the heart of the universe opens to us and we eventually see all "through the eyes of love" as my song suggests:

> "When I see through the eyes of love,
> There's no place to lay the blame.
> When I see through the eyes of love,
> Saint and sinner are the same."

This place of non-judgment of our self or another is the main preparation for what we call a "happy death". The soul in us longs for us to be able to see life as a river flowing from one state of consciousness to another, to see each state as a preparation for the next. Michelangelo's "The Return of the Prodigal" is for me symbolic of what Celtic consciousness names, "calling all of ourselves home". Michelangelo's artwork depicts the younger son coming home to the house of the Father and the Father blessing him in welcome. When I can welcome all of me, the lost prodigal parts—i.e., the parts that have so-called left home, have squandered the inheritance of love, have wandered out there, the confused foolish self, the arrogant and self-absorbed self, the parts I have placed on the shoulders of others because they were too heavy for me to own—when I can welcome them all home to my own hearth and warm them at the fires of my own self-compassion, then I can begin to see the world through the eyes of love and not through those of condemnation.

The Celtic idea of calling ourselves home is all about our relationship with our soul-self. From the beginning of time, the soul calls the clay body in us alive. The calling of us in from the outer world suggests a deep longing in our souls to *Beidh ag teacht abhaile a grá*: Come home, beloved; come home to the love that has never forsaken you, never left your house, never blamed or sent you away. This calling ourselves home is symbolic of the longing for belonging that throbs in the hearts of men and women, that drums our feet to our own pastures in the end: "Come home, dear love, come home." Imagine welcoming yourself in with the words of this song.

> Welcome, welcome, child of the Universe
> Welcome, welcome to this place
> Welcome, welcome, child of the Universe
> We have waited for your beauty and your grace

Never-Ending Life

Since time immemorial our tribal ancestors, including the Celts and later Celtic Christians, believed that life does not end. It cannot. Life has been and ever will flow in and through us whether in form or out of form. We have been forever and ever and we will go on forever and ever. There is no death, no ending and no getting out of life whether we are in earth or in spirit. We enter into earth as a material expression of life; we leave this form behind at a certain time and enter into another way of life that is spirit. We are not only the offspring of life itself, true images of our eternal mighty creator; this boundless force chooses us to image itself on earth and in spirit.

Life is no respecter of expression. The Celts believed that it breathes out and worlds of creation pour out, scattering particles of life everywhere. If you take a walk in the woods you will see such a scattering—life in the trees and life in the so-called dead leaves you walk on. Life scatters clouds to dance the sky alive. The very air you breathe tingles with this powerful source.

If we replace the word "death" with the word "transition", we may be better able to see the hand of the great magician all around without the usual connotations of dreadful endings. Life is the great transformer, the great alchemist, everything in its own good time, and this transformation or metamorphosis is alive with the energy of the Creator or *Tobar beatha*, from the Gaelic, meaning "well of life".

I would like us to take a momentary look at the process called incarnation and see if we can adopt the same procedure for the dying process. If we consider incarnation as a physical act only we totally miss out on the magnitude of the drama of ascent. I believe that this mystery of becoming happens on myriad levels, too complex and too wondrous for us earth-minded humans to understand. I will, however, very simply explain the idea of transmigration according to our ancestors, the Celts.

It is given in the "Teachings from the Cauldron" that, before the soul "in-bodies", it makes a contract or a promise with spirit, to reach a certain spiritual maturity or evolution before it returns to spirit-life again. The main work of the soul is in integrating the earth-mind into the mind of the creator, thus spiritualizing it; the task is to put an end to dualism and bringing it back to a place of love.

The earth-mind cannot love unconditionally; it has to be purified, transformed in the Cauldron of Immortality, in the fire of Brigit.

Seemingly, the earth-mind is essential to enlightenment without which we cannot reach liberation. The soul uses our human experiences to achieve this. Most religions believe that the earth-mind or ego-mind is evil, thus unworthy of compassionate attention, and suggest various methods of controlling and conquering it. Our Celtic ancestors, however, deem it worthy of acknowledgement as it represents our animal nature, which is instinctive and helps us to survive on the earth. Thus they related to it without fear and many stories of the gods and goddesses stirring together the dark and light, day and night, birth and death, good and evil were later regarded as grist to the mill of Celtic psychological folklore.

It would appear that the contract to become human necessitates three so-called deaths (changes):

Alchemical Action	Transforming Action	Result
Death to life in spirit	Ascent to form	Conception
Death to life in womb	Emergence from womb	Birth
Death to life in form	Detachment from form	Death

The contract to become human would also necessitate three so-called births (changes):

Alchemical Action	Transforming Action	Result
Birth from life in spirit	Ascent to form	Conception
Birth from life in womb	Emergence from womb	Birth
Birth from life in form	Detachment from form	Death

It is about coming into and going into. The Celtic spiral of life, death, life. In the Gaelic, *Ag dul amach ag dul isteach*, it is about transcending. It is about movement and change and letting go of one experience in order to enter fully into another just as mysterious. It is about "closing this door behind". It is a dance, a totally divinely inspired flamenco of colours with the accompaniment of the music of the cosmos to breathe through. That is all, and all is total mystery and miracle and we poor humans try to unravel the mystery and we cannot. Nor are we supposed to. Here we enter into the world of paradox. Here the soul feels at home. Here the Divine reigns supremely in that expansive and all-embracing Cauldron of Divine Wisdom.

The times and the ways in which scenes from this great drama are revealed depend on the willingness of our souls to receive such instructions without analyzing or structuring them into a neatly formed theology. The imparting of such knowledge is called inspiration which, as Jesus the Christ advised, was revealed to children and not to the worldly wise. The Celts called it *fios*, i.e., to know without the help of external data—what we today call intuitive knowing from the soul's remembering. It would seem that in the world of spirit, timing or awareness is all-important… yet there is no such phenomenon as time within its all-pervading breath. Brigit the Goddess called time, "the conscious rhythms of our soul, the poetry of watchfulness".

This is difficult for us to grasp as we dedicate so much of our energy to chronological time watching. In spirit world or *Tir-na-nÓg*, everything happens in the great Now where past and future unite to form the great all-pervading presence. In this presence, all creation has been set in motion, and is orderly and clearly defined from a place of all-knowing and all-acceptance, therefore nothing is left to chance or maybe. Nothing and no one is judged or deemed an outsider.

Nothing is accidental and nothing happens at the so-called "wrong time". In spirit world, nothing is insignificant. Not even a sparrow falls without notice and even the hairs on our head are counted. With respect to birth, the exquisite nature of spirit respects all expressions of itself in all form. Regarding human form, it matters not whether the soul, which is the messenger of spirit, lives in the earth-plane for many years or has contracted to come only to experience the confinement of the womb-space and leave again. It may choose to remain on earth for some time in the limitations of a handicapped body. All embodiments are graced with mystery and acknowledged as sacred as each birth, and consequently each death, carries within it the consciousness of the Divine, which is life itself.

couchinꞇ che liꞙe ꞙorce

This is an exercise you can do anywhere in nature. Take a friend with you for support, especially if you do this for the first time; the turning might make you dizzy. If your dog or cat are close by, they will love it.

NOTE: If you have high blood pressure, do the spinning very slowly and with your eyes open. I would not recommend this exercise if you suffer from vertigo.

Throughout the exercise I suggest you do what I call the "snoring breath". In Yogic terms, it is called oojay breathing and goes as follows:

Find a comfortable place in nature.

Stand and relax the body/mind.

Breathe in deeply with the sound of a snore.

Now breathe out slowly, as if pushing the breath out through the nose from the back of the throat. Continue breathing in this way.

Widen your arms away from your sides.

Half close your eyes.

Spin around slowly in a clockwise direction approximately six times. (If you have high blood pressure, do it very slowly and with your eyes open.)

Stop if you feel dizzy!

Stand still and draw your arms closer together for a moment so that they are out-stretched in front of you.

Place your hands over your shut eyes.

Sense what is happening and breathe slowly.
What you are experiencing is the exaggerated flow of life force rushing through the whole of your body/mind.

When the sensations settle, take your hands away.
Now, open your eyes to whatever natural scene is directly in front of you.

Give it your full concentration and breathe in fully.
Keep gazing until you feel the dance you create together.
You become one with this energy.

This is life force (source) that is flowing. You become one with all nature which is spirit. Your essence is spirit, the essence of the tree or the sky or the flower is also spirit. You are not separate from that which you breathe with and you breathe life itself.

Now, go round anticlockwise once and do as directed above.

Feel the energy vibrating around you.

Feel your unsteadiness as you hold to the earth.

Open your eyes and see what you perceive.

Now rest.

Do this little exercise often if it suits you. (It is helpful in times of depression, when you feel detached from the world.)

This is a kind of letting-go experience. This is what many people describe as out-of-body sensations when they let go of earth. All will be in a flow of colour, as you will feel the colours of your own energy centres and the sound of their individual musical notes creating buzzing sounds in your consciousness. Imagine if you did not have to try and steady yourself but could go with the flow until you eventually become the flow of colour and sound and vibration.

Imagine you would be absorbed into the all-spiralling vortex, just going with the heightened vibrations (the dizziness exaggerated) until you simply are taken into the vast expanse of nature herself, having let the breath merge with hers, having let your spirit merge with the Great Spirit itself without the fear which makes us hold on. This would indeed be symbolic of opening into life and death. This would be the beginning of that journey at the end of which is what the poet called "that quiet rest". And that quiet rest is the all absorbing energy of pure love.

Death as Mystery
in the Celtic Tradition

The Celtic mind never spoke of the theological history of death; rather it spoke of the mysteries within it. I love the word "mystery" for it holds at its core the great "story" of our lives here in the earth and in spirit. Each person has her/his own story. Each story is full of mystery with adventure, and each adventure is unique *to the storyteller*. The Irish have a saying:

> "Mo sceal fein, sceal gach duine
> Ach is ionam fein a bhfuil an sceal."

Translated, this means: "My story and yours are the same, but it is within my-self (soul) that my story lives." This means my story never dies; my story is not finished with the completion of earth life. Even when we have ceased to "in-body" our life, our story persists in another dimension. No matter how similar the stories may appear in earth form, no two lives are really the same, as no two people have the same assignment on earth to carry out. Often when two people meet and exchange stories and see the similarity of events and situations in both their lives, they begin to bond, as the belief is that they are both on the same journey. They may be disappointed later to realize that, although the events and traumas may have been similar, the teachings in them have not. We are each of us on a sole (soul) journey in the earth and often we meet like-minded souls and we happily travel together for a part of the journey. Whilst the reality is that we are alone, our relationship to other created phenomena is important; they hold a key to our own unconscious, our *Anam-Cara*, soul-friend on the journey to our self. If, as our Celtic ancestors believed, we are one with all natural phenomena, then one may deduce that the same life source flows eternally through all. The Celts honoured the animal kingdom as they did the plants and grasses. Cuchulainn's name translates as "the hound of Cullainn". Cernunnos, the "Horned God" king of the animal world, ruled the kingdoms of giving and receiving, life and death, in an everflowing cycle.

This identification with the animals brought human beings closer to their own *animas* (souls), their own earthedness and mystery. It also assisted their skills in nonverbal communication. They learnt the mysterious symbolic language of life and death from nature and especially from the animals. This language translated into the fluent continuum of myths and legends, which connected all life—the life of the so-called inanimate, animal, and plant kingdoms. The animals showed us how important our instinctual selves are. How whenever we do not listen to the first three energy centres in our form and learn from the important information held there, we become ungrounded in our so-called spirituality and too quickly try to access the higher vibrations. This does not lead to wholeness.

The "Teachings from the Cauldron", and most ancient beliefs, taught that we live out our lives in a continuous cycle of incarnating and excarnating. The Celts associated incarnating with a seductive sound or call from the soul into the clay body of forgetfulness and excarnating with a sound or call from the soul into the spirit of remembrance again. Here I will summarize in a very simplified and non-theological manner what this calling forth means according to the "Teachings from the Cauldron":

Incarnation as a Call to
embodiment . . . inspiration
anticipation of experiences
attraction to an earth-mind
cathexis (i.e., the concentration of mental/emotional energy in one channel or object)
limited consciousness

Excarnation as a Call to
disembodiment . . . expiration
completion of experiences
de-cathexis from earth-mind
limitless consciousness

This may be an arrogant way to attempt to describe the greatest mystery that could possibly occur and yet we have continued our arrogance in trying to comprehend the stories of life and death since time began. For the Celts, the mysteries of life in its comings and goings were enacted through the medium of theatre, verse, song and storytelling. The *Filid*, or bards, who were the Master poets and verse speakers told the many myths and *Scéalta* (stories).

The male warriors liked to sit together under the oak tree and talk about their courage in battles, where death itself was an invited component and part of the ritual, for which there was much preparation both external and internal. Many stories were told of the Celtic god, Lugh, father of the great warrior, Cuchulainn. He was skilled in the art of battle and was said to have victory over death. Later known as the triple god, he carried within his persona the attributes of the Roman gods Mercury, Apollo and Mars. Translated, his name means "Lightning" which may correspond to his alert, quick mind and body. This quickness also assisted his travel through the worlds of creation.

The *Seábheans*, or old wise women, around the hearth fire told the less physically active stories, the more spiritual aspects of death and dying, in the winter nights. Before they told the stories, they invited death to sit by the fire also and listen to the tales told about her! In modern psychology, this is known as integrating the shadow. I remember as a child listening to the old ones telling stories about how death came as "a friendly creature" to the old woman who was "too old to bother speaking any more" or how "the breath of death was in him", referring to an old man who "couldn't lift his hand to the whiskey bottle any more". Death was seen as a compassionate friend who released the soul to rest. These and many other stories of death were told in the darkness of the room with only an oil lamp giving eerie light in the corner of the window, thus adding to the mystery. I often think that Carl G. Jung would have borrowed some of my grandmother's sayings had they met! Her advice to me one time, when I was afraid to go into the "room at the top of the stairs" for fear of its being haunted, was full of sound, Jungian wisdom: "If you don't go into the dark rooms on your own, the devils will haul you in by the heels."

This was a wonderful way of helping me to integrate the shadow!

A Time for Change

Ah the start

Now the end

Ah the welcome

Now the goodbye

Ah the joy

Now the sorrow

So is life

So is death

So is life

Death was ever-present in the psyches of the Celts. They had an innate need to release whatever served them no longer and to welcome the new as one would welcome a guest. The old Irish *Seábhean* or wise woman used to say "welcome beginnings and endings as neighbours to the house".

They seemed to be able to see the flow between the worlds and because of their belief in the "story", they were no strangers to mystery and awe. Each season brought its own transformation and they coincided with the internal changes within their own psyches. This close connection with nature helped our Celtic relations to see that there was a "time for all things under heaven". There was a time for warring and a time for peace, a time to sing and a time to mourn. They did not forget the earth that connected them with their spirits. The honouring of death as the releaser of the past is seen in many Celtic rituals, especially their rituals around *Samhain* which took place at the end of October and is now known as "Halloween" or "Holy evening". This was the time when the harvest was safely gathered in and the old year was released with joy. Death was not the enemy. Our ancestors expressed their lives fully and ritualistically in the present. The springtime of their lives was celebrated as were the summer, autumn, and winter. "Each season has her own story," my grandmother would say, with a knowing in her eyes that told many stories. Our inheritance is one of tremendous integrity, of being able to be in the natural way of things with a gentle willingness to re-lease and greet the next moment. The more we get together, tell the stories, and share our losses, the more we deal with our daily letting-go, the better able we will be to meet with death, our own death. Then we will see it for what it is—a natural state of life, not the end of a life but the transforming of one type of being into another.

Most of us are unwilling to look at the subject of death and dying: *our* death and *our* dying. It is difficult to deal with the thoughts of our own demise; the best we seem able to do is to cope with it. How easy to deny even the so-called small deaths in our everyday lives. They are but reminders of that final letting-go of all, the final out-breath. When we are unwilling to let go and grieve the small deaths—little goodbyes, losses—we become more and more attached to things as they were and mostly live in the past.

Being human is synonymous with change, growth, instability, and insecurity. Psychologically, physiologically, mentally, and emotionally the human psyche is forever in flux. Nature herself, who was the great mentor for the Celts, is not static but *ecstatic* and her movements are always towards balance and growth. The leaves that fall in autumn provide nourishment for the earth. Nothing is wasted. Yet, we are so full of fear: fear of loss. The Celts believed in the whole concept of sacrifice; it had a different meaning from the self-deprecation, the self-martyrdom with which we view it. They saw it as one variable giving way to another, a letting-go in order to recreate. They had no fear of death. The soul was at home with the dark: "When we do not willingly look at our death shadow, the shadow overshadows us."

The darkness of our fears becomes the shadow, the monster. The darkness here is the inability to accept the inevitability of change. When we do not know the end of the story it is difficult to feel secure. Here are words that carry this meaning well:

"I will not judge the appearance of this loss

Because I do not know its story

But I will grieve no matter what the cost,

Surrendering yesterday's glory.

My heart will open wider to my soul

And sweet compassion gently holds me.

And then one day my story will be told

And joy will fill the empty spaces

As my life wondrously unfolds

With wings of light I will embrace it."

We can never really see the whole story of our lives. In retrospect, situations which we judged tragic or heartbreaking may reveal a whole different story. We can see the way in which our souls have guided us towards the deeper opening of our hearts. The Cauldron teaches that the soul in us uses each situation to stretch our heart's capacity to love more universally.

The Story of Dying and Celtic Beliefs

The Celts believed in the transmigration of souls. They believed there was a magical rhythm and a particular order to this transmigration. The Gaelic word *Trasna* describes this well. *Trasna* means to consciously cross over, to be at the crossroads of shape-change, to come to the end of something and to move organically into the re-forming, of the next form. What are the transformations that take place within our clay as the soul in us prepares to leave its temporary home? How can one possibly draw the curtain that separates the world of spirit from the world of form? We are as blind women and men with walking sticks, treading on very insecure ground, when we arrogantly believe we can know anything empirically at all. What we need to do is move into our *anima*, our animal presence, and listen with our eyes and see with our ears. We have to be able to tell stories, stories of death and life. We have to be able to smell stories before telling them; we have only to be willing to open our mouth, and the stories then tell themselves. This is how our ancestors grew in wisdom's ways. This is how theories were begotten. They spoke in symbols and told stories to explain the wonders and magnitude of the earth in which they lived. Jesus the Christ did likewise; he relied on stories as a means of teaching. The old ones believed that the storytellers were alchemists who held within them the ability to take raw, inspirational words and change them into living embers which burn and grow within the psyche of the listener, who in turn adds to the story in the retelling of it. Thus the story becomes a living entity, not just dead words. And a story also expands as it is told and retold. My story told by me, must of course be different to my story as witnessed and retold by another. They will include their individual experiences of me in a way I cannot and vice versa.

If we rely on scientific enquiry for our information, regarding the continuance of life after death of the body, we know it cannot produce hard empirical evidence, even though we have many records of people who have experienced near-death experiences. What I share with you is what I have experienced in my own life, from listening to the inner stories from my ancestors and from my own subjective account of out-of-body experiences.

One such out of body experience happened in 1973 in Northern Ireland. I had a visit from a friend I hadn't seen for a while and she had brought her very young baby with her. My first child Anthea was two years at the time, and we lived in an upstairs flat. During her visit, she noticed a smell coming from the kitchen across the way, and when I went to investigate, the electric cooker seemed to be in flame. I had left the chip pan on high, and it had burnt dry. In a panic, I went to the mains to turn off the electric and touched live wires. The result was electrocution. They tell me I fell and bumped my head in panic to reach my friend and the children in the living room.

Somehow they got themselves downstairs, and I remember a priest standing over me giving me the last rights. Strangely enough I "saw" Anthea being taken to a neighbour's house, and I was happy that she was okay. I did not know what happened to my friend, but obviously she was taken to a safe place. I could see what was happening all around me in the hospital, and noticed how the nurses panicked. Yet, I was fine, I was floating away from it all. In this inner space of pure ease and beauty, I was absorbed into the most exquisite music and colours which danced in the music. Whilst I did not see any Beings, I felt impressed by a presence that was both authoritarian and kind. The words, "You cannot learn anything you don't already know" seemed to fill my being and I again was impressed with the sentence "You need not read spiritual books, you need not search for truth, you need not find a teacher. As you need to know, you will know. There is a knowledge of which you know not right now, but as you grow in soul-full awareness, all will be made known to you."

This encounter with otherliness was interrupted by the sound of my husband crying at my bedside. I knew I had to come back. I knew I had to experience more of life on earth. I had to spend time in the Cauldron so that I would teach from experience and not from books. This NDE was a kindness offered me at a time when life in Northern Ireland and my personal experiences in my marriage were near unbearable. It is good and kind that life offers us one breath at a time. And that we do not see our futures.

Trying to adjust to everyday life in Northern Ireland after that was excruciating; nothing seemed real. I didn't seem real. With no help, other than tranquilizers to help my poor body-mind to half engage in this painful so-called normal life, I felt not fully incarnated. Because of the trauma, every bomb, every gun shot, every angry outburst from the television left me feeling wrecked. Thankfully, for Anthea, Granny and Granda were a great help in minding her. Her beautiful Being, her very presence, her curly blond hair, all gave me reasons to stay, thank you, Anthea.

Since this NDE, my life seemed to take a different turn. And ten years later to the month I met Elisabeth Kübler-Ross, M.D. But I had been working with the dying in Northern Ireland before that, and Elizabeth verified for me, that death is a natural phenomenon, and life is not diminished by death.

Death, the Great Catalyst

It would seem that there is an art of dying as there is of living. As there is a biology operating during life to ensure that the life force stays attached to the earth body, so also there is a biology which ensures that the same life force naturally detaches itself from the body in the process of dying. All the ancient teachings seem to insist that a great drama takes place during the last days of a life on earth. Alice Bailey named death "the great adventure" whilst the Celtic, Egyptian and American Indian cultures viewed dying as a preparation for a great journey. I have certainly concluded that the dying person is not just lying there with nothing happening. It is undeniable that the most profound and meaningful journey is taking place and only the person dying can experience its magnitude. No one can truly describe what death is like, as there is no language for miracle, and maybe that is just the way it is meant to be from the beginning. If there were no death, we could not continue our healing journey to ourselves. We need a catalyst, a loving, non-judgmental catalyst to provide a space for our story to continue.

No one has come from the place of mystery to tell us what their final resting place is like. Moreover, if they did, it would be just one story out of billions. Therefore, we have to be content with much speculation, intuitive knowing, accounts of near-death experiences, stories from good reliable mediums, scientific research into the physiology of dying and our own spiritual beliefs.

The Celts had many stories relating to death and the magical places one may visit in the upper worlds or lower worlds. In order to partake fully of the wonders to be enjoyed in the upper worlds, one had to do many earth trips so that with each trip one "could leave part of the old garment behind and at last, put on the cloak of gold". Reincarnation was a tenet of their beliefs due to their Indo-European legacy. I personally believe that this rich inheritance also influenced their music, and the colourful soul Sanskrit language formed a nucleus for what we term the old pre-Anglicized Gaelic language. Celtic Christians also held reincarnation as a tenet of belief up until the 6th century. It is as if the spiral of life was a natural phenomenon evident in all creation.

Shape-Changing

Stories of shape-changing show the way in which a human being could change into an animal or bird in order either to overpower another to set right an old rift, or for the purpose of gaining wisdom innate to the particular bird or animal. Fintan, Celtic warrior, shape-changed into a salmon, eagle and hawk in order to free himself from earth density. The outward transformation resulted in the inward of transformed identity. The Welsh goddess Cerridwen, who was the keeper of the Cauldron of the Underworld, changed into many animal figures in order to find her son. Eventually, she changed into a hen and ate the ear of corn into which her son had been transformed. This is also representative of death, the old Crone, or old woman eating up youth. Stories where humans transformed themselves into animals and later into gods, shows the interrelationship between the *Anima* and spirit.

It would seem that we also have to undergo shape-changing albeit in a less dramatic physical way so that we can adapt to the energies of the world of spirit. If we have not "shape-changed" our internal awareness, or earth-mind, to enable this transformation to occur, our time of final initiation will be less blissful. According to our Celtic ancestors, we all have a chance to reincarnate or shape-change at least five times during one lifetime. Each time we make a complete leap of faith, or transform our thinking so radically as to seem to be a completely new, different person, it is believed that we have shape-changed. This can happen through illness or when we have had a trauma or great loss in our lives.

changing beliefs

Name the occasions in your life when you changed your beliefs about something important.

What changes have you made regarding your beliefs about spirituality in the past ten years?

What changes have you made regarding your beliefs about the next life?

Do you believe that change is part of being alive?

Share your answers with a friend and discuss the subject matter with them.

The Celts believed that we are all interconnected and I believe in the old Irish proverb:

"Is ar scath a chéile a mhaireann na daoine."

["In the shadow of each other we live."]

A New Language

All around us in our universe are manifestations of greatness and majesty, which our finite minds cannot possibly comprehend. "The unfinished universe" emphasizes the miracle that surrounds each new scientific finding. In an attempt to explain created phenomena and the evolutionary cycles to be found therein, scientists need to learn a new language: the language of soul. These cycles that expand the whole story of evolution from so-called inanimate matter to human can no longer be explained away in an arid intellectual context. The scientist has to learn from the storyteller in order to reach the heart of mystery. How can one explain evolution without the use of words like compassion, spirit, love? Likewise, the storyteller has to be able to incorporate concepts such as hypotheses, alchemy and metamorphosis if they are to put bones to, or earth, a story.

Overall, we are but children playing around in the house of creation, unaware of the magnificence and unbelievable splendour all around us. We are connected to all the worlds of creation; therefore some of us occasionally see through the veils that separate us and become inspired by what is revealed to us in those sacred moments of stillness. I am aware, however, that not all information that comes to us from "the other side" is necessarily true and honourable.

Being born into the world of matter appears similar to being born into the world of immaterialism. Both would seem to include great challenges. These include struggle, fear, confusion, hard work and hopefully a sense of achievement. If we could know the struggles, the "my-stories" (mysteries), the self-mercy or self-hate, the insights and clarity, the fears and the relief that the dying person experiences, we would appreciate more the need for silence, respect, prayers and intercessions. As we approach death, we become more and more aware of our internal worlds, and our de-cathexis from the world of form and physicality happens gradually. We have to internalize the external world; we have to find a home for all created phenomena to include our animal natures with the self . . .

When people are very ill, they are not sure if they will complete the whole journey, i.e., if they will actually die. This may be a forerunner and proper death may happen in a few years. So many, myself included, have been very near death and have returned into the body again as we had not gone to the second *Áite* (Gaelic for "state" or "place"), or *Bardo* in Tibetan. The pain of resuscitation can be quite unnerving for many. They do not want body life again; they wish to remain in their "shape-changed" energy, but the soul knows exactly why it is necessary to come back to earth form. I believe I had not fully incarnated into this body and had to come back to do so. Mostly, such people like me have chosen difficult incarnations this time around and have an unconscious wish or longing to go home. The compassionate soul allows the situation to occur where the person experiences an out-of-body space, a shape-change, where they can enjoy a deep rest and re-experience unconditional love. I feel I tapped into knowledge that later helped me in times of deep pain and stress. Once we experience the power of unconditional love, we can face anything in life.

Elisabeth Kübler-Ross, M.D., taught that when a person has an NDE, they are never afraid of dying thereafter, as they realize that consciousness or life is continuous and nothing is ever lost. This is in keeping with the beliefs our ancestors held. The more we can let go and surrender to our soul's love, the more we can accept the shape-changing of death. In my NDE I was allowed to experience pure love. I believe that this experience showed me that when we unite again or at least come close again to this love we remember what we are. And this knowledge creates a sense of inner knowing. We remember for a short time, the love that we are and the separation is healed. I believe that orgasm is also a near-death experience that creates unity consciousness and the two beings become one in love.

changing form

What are your fears about dying?

What shape-changes in your body/mind are difficult for you to accept?

How do you "deal" as opposed to "cope" with change in your days?

If you could ask a dying person one question, what might it be?

Write down these answers and share your feelings and thoughts with a friend. Invite her/him to do likewise.

Being able to adapt to the seasons of the heart without losing our centre is of great importance when we are faced with death—our own and others. Get used to recognizing that still small voice that sings in you when something needs to be changed, renewed, or let go of. It will then be automatic for you when death comes. Many people are stuck in a place of so-called ease—comfort, non-risk taking, so-called security—so that it is difficult for them to make that shape-change from body life to spirit life: as within so without. The dear old ego heart is so scared of change because it sees death as annihilation; it does not know that the transformation can be glorious and very wondrous. How can it know? It only knows about fear and punishment regarding death. Is that not what it has learnt? What an amazing shock for the dear ego! It will have to surrender to love and if it has not done so before death, it will be more difficult later on. One thing that is essential to know is that "love (soul) alone can heal the ego, as love alone can transform its fear".

The *Áite*, or Passages of Birth and Death

The word *Áite* is the Gaelic equivalent of the Tibetan *Bardo*; it means "passageway" or "state of consciousness". Both words have their roots in Sanskrit. In the Celtic tradition, it is used to describe the birthing process as well as the dying process. In the following pages, I will lead you into the Áite of Birth and Death and to the relevance of the Death Áite for our lives today.

It was whilst I was "watching" with a person dying some years ago that I remembered how my old Nanny used to pray for the souls in purgatory and limbo. She said it was our duty to "get them out" so that they could "go on to heaven". The Catholic Church recommended that we offer prayers and that we fast on the 2nd November every year for the release of these dear souls.

One night, not long after this reminiscence, I was shown quite clearly where the souls go who have not had time to prepare for death or who have committed suicide. I seemed to travel at an enormous speed within myself and was shocked and sad at what I saw along the way. The same night I was shown how our misdeeds or thoughts of unlove create a mist or fog of darkness within our bodies and the actual place we live and how this darkness becomes dense until it becomes an entity. I was shown different countries where wars and violence took place and I felt sick with the slime of dark filth that met my eyes. Naturally I thought it was my own inner shadows that needed to be released into the light of love. I worked on this and challenged my own soul if I was holding on to some revenge or unlove for myself or another and still the scene remained unchanged.

At last, I asked if I might help in some way. The answer was clear—yes, I could help. When I agreed to do so in whatever way possible, I then was given rituals and prayers of release to perform. The Incantation (see later) is one such prayer that I wrote down immediately and I have not changed it in any way since I received it. I was told distinctly that I had the ability, since childhood, to travel with the soul that was dying and could help it through intercessions and rituals until it had met with its own guardians. These spirits would then transport the soul to the light. Although seeing the pain and suffering of the dear souls who could not accept love and light was quite horrific, I was relieved to have been shown also the immense joy and bliss enjoyed by the souls who leave the earth in surrender to love or God or whatever they call spirit. To name this place of pure love is not possible for we have no such concepts; enough to say that we meet with the essence of love itself, our own divinity, and that is untainted joy.

I was given insights into the Birthing rites also and they were so real for me that I could feel the soul experiencing the actual birth in such a welcoming setting. I also felt the relief of the soul returning to spirit having spent a short while in earthed form. Each state of being in life was perfect: all was orderly. The death of a baby is very painful for parents yet this sad loss can be the foundation for strengthening parents as they actively grieve together. The birth of a so-called physically or mentally handicapped child seems tragic to our small minds, yet, to the initiated, these births are precious lives in themselves, carrying out their own specific contracts, and act as great catalysts for parents and others.

Whilst I do not have permission to teach you all of the above-mentioned rituals and intercessions—as one must teach them orally—I am, however, honoured and humbled to present you with the following ritual in the name of love.

NOTE: This ritual is not to be done by those who are attached to the dead person, or have any emotional attachment, or desired outcome. This ritual is done with neutral love, which is compassion, and with an inner authority that is humbled by grace.

The Ritual and Incantation

DIA ÓN ÁIT SEO

Life energy is leaving this space. (By life energy we mean the energy to stay in form.)

1. You are alone with the dead person in the room, standing at the right side of the bed.

2. Go slowly into the presence within yourself, letting the breath take you there. Your heart is gentled into a space of clarity, needing nothing from the outcome.

3.   Take a deep in-breath, place both hands above the feet of the dead person, never touching the body or the clothes. Let the words *"DIA ÓN ÁIT SEO"* be slowly chanted.

4.   Moving up the body, again repeat *"DIA ÓN ÁIT SEO"* where you feel uneasiness under your hands and in your own belly, pause. Repeat the incantation. Stay there with hands poised, repeating the incantation until you feel the release.

5.   When you reach the heart-centre, feel a connection with a deeper compassion, unemotional and devotional. Repeat *"DIA ÓN ÁIT SEO"* as the conditioned love within the being of the dead person is transformed into the universal heart.

6.   Let the hands flow to the top of the head and out of the top of the head, into the ether.

7.   Remain there quietly readjusting to the universal heart within yourself. The vibrations now in the room have heightened, and a deep peace will descend. This peace is palpable, the soul has done the work of releasing, in so far as you can allow yourself to be a sacred harp through which the graces of divine love can flow, you will be blessed in this ritual. *Seá.*

The trajectory of the hand movements suggests the energy leaving from the feet, which is earth energy, and out the top of the head, representing time and space. When I suggest above that you leave the hands on an area until you feel a release, what is happening is that you are sensing old blocked energy in that energy field. A sacred thought at this stage is *"That too is released into love"*. If the person had lived a Christian life, I would add the words *"That too is forgiven"*. So the full movement is about releasing earth energy including static energy.

The *Áite* of Birth

When the potential parents felt it was time to procreate, they approached the various wise people in the tribe for support and advice. This advice usually came in the person of the astrologer, who was usually one of the druids; a *Fili*, who was a master storyteller and poet; a wise woman, usually a Crone; and the oldest man and woman. They each advised from their own particular perspective.

The First *Áite* of Birth
Earthing the Seed in the Cave

Sexuality was synonymous with spirituality in the times of our Celtic forebears. As spirituality was derived from earth religions and the feminine was respected as the great creative force in all the worlds, sexuality was seen as holy and, therefore, celebrated. The sexual act was deemed sacred and was a powerful force where the woman's body was adored and honoured as the great image of Goddess.

When the female and male were ready for hand-fasting or marriage, they were instructed by the elders regarding the sexual rites of passage for the male and female. Usually, the men educated the males and the women instructed the women. If the man were a virgin, he would be circumcized, as a cleansing ritual. It was a custom for a person to have more than one partner and the children were loved by the extended family. Homosexual people seemingly refrained from this particular expression of love but they formed a large, important part of the assembly of poets, storytellers, astrologers, artists, singers and creative ritual makers. They created in a different way. Great care was taken to ensure that the ambience was an inviting one to celebrate the earthing of the seed. The chamber was decorated with flowers and sweet grasses, candles were lit, and the couple consciously came together in love. The young man had learned how to make sure the seed was planted deep into the waiting womb and, when the act of love was over, they again consciously gave thanks and welcomed the new life force that had asked to be birthed. This welcome helped to create a space of joy for the coming life. (To welcome was natural for our ancestors.) It was a custom for many of the people in the community to gather outside the chamber in anticipation of things to come. When the sound of the completion of the act of love was over, they would offer thanksgiving to the great gods and goddesses of life and death. The love call then went out to the life force and it began the journey of earthing. (If the couple had both been virgins, the bloods from the hymen and from the circumcision were mixed together and placed in earth, thus symbolizing the earthing of the life force.) The old stories tell us that the awaiting soul hovers around the aura of the mother for at least three months before conception. It is said, too, that the potential mother knows if the planting has taken place inside her for she has *Glóire an Anam*, the honouring of the soul, around her. For the first three months, she has magic powers, especially in the way of divining for water and in hearing the song of trees and rivers. It is also said that she can breathe on the dead and bring them to life, if she so desires. (Brigit is the giver of this grace.)

The Second *Áite* of Birth
The Coming In of the *Beatha*, or Life

The third month was an important time for the young life, as this was the time when soul and body united in love. It is said that the heart of the child beats more strongly when this happens. The heart now begins to tune into its own rhythms and begins to settle into the ways of the growing organism. Many mothers feel a subtle difference take place after the third month. They speak of a cessation of sickness, which they sometimes would have felt in the mornings upon awakening. The young life force begins to stretch itself into the space provided in the womb, but it has only limited room for movement. Therefore it feels confined, cramped and smothered. The soul, by definition, is expansive and whilst needing a body with which to experience itself fully cannot do so as yet. (The same process happens at death when the soul needs to magnify its consciousness and experience a world of other sounds, colours, and movements; it needs to feel spaciousness.)

The last 28 days are days of gathering energy, sensations of loss and excitement. This time also opens to sensing the mother's emotions, her apprehension and fears, her grief and loss around the imminent birth. There is a need for the child to undergo a process of de-cathexis from the mother before birth, so they both experience the grief of separation and pending joy of new life. (The Cauldron teaches that 28 days prior to dying we also go through these emotions or sensations trying to decathex from the physical life, needing to give all our energy to the process of dying.)

The old ones believed that the new life force experiences many different sensations—for instance, needing to separate from the mother yet needing to be with her—so there is much grief and confusion. Seemingly, a male life force finds it more difficult to separate than a female. It would seem in many cases that the male child clings to the mother, needing her attention much more than his female counterpart does.

The Third *Áite* of Birth
The Flowing Mountain

The mother was advised to keep moving until the delivery of her child. At no time was she told to lie down, as this was deemed unnatural. The child had to be dropped to earth, not dragged out (at death, according to Tibetan Buddhists, the body is dropped to the earth). The potential mother did not have to celebrate any special rituals other than be in touch with the new life force with love and ease, showing it the beauty of nature through her eyes.

The mother was massaged with various oils and was given certain herbs to eat and drink to facilitate the birth. Her partner sang to the life force, enticing it to life and to an easy passage. Mantras were repeated to the life force daily in a low key, so that the soul might be attracted to the earth plane.

Water was a very sacred element according to the Celtic people. The outpouring of the waters from the womb of the mother was called "the flowing fountain", suggesting purification and a heralder of new life.

At birth the new life force had to go through the so-called "dark tunnel" (the cervix) and through the "outer chamber" (vagina), in order to come into the world. Emerging from the ethereal body, the new soul needed to ground itself and did so by means of concentrated energy in the base of the body, by means of *An Corda Geal*, the silver cord or spiritual umbilical. It replaced the physical umbilical when the child came into the world and it brought the other energy spirals with it. Its work was to establish each energy spiral in its located place around the body-mind before birth. The red terracotta of the base spiral hooked into the anus of the child and earthed itself. The soul was attracted to this place of *fire* energy. It was like a magnet to the new life form and the soul put all its power into this descent.

With the assistance of the *Corda Geal*, the other spirals took up their place along the spine. The child felt this rush or flow of colours as the orange, yellow, turquoise, magenta and violet colours all engaged themselves in the physical beingness. The *Corda Geal* settled at the top of the head, the pulsating of which did not stop until the energy spirals were in situ. This usually happened three months after birth, as the young child was still adjusting to earth existence. Thus, the vital endocrine or glandular systems of the body were ready for activation in the child's body.

The Fourth *Áite* of Birth
The Warm Wind

The first in-breath was all-important. It was the bridge to new life in the world of matter. Often the child took her first breath as her head emerged from the cave or womb. It sometimes happened, though, that the child's lungs had to be cleared of mucus before it could breathe. When the in-breath happened, then the attending family knew that the new life form could survive alone. They began to chant another welcome chant:

"Welcome, welcome, welcome

To the newborn child of grace,

We know the beauty of

The earth in the radiance of Your face."

They laid the child on the belly of the mother, who laid in the arms of three other mothers who were her helpers in encouraging the child to birth. The father, always near the mother as her primary support, took the child and, with his mouth on the child's head and forehead, gave it the breath of life. The welcoming chant for the child to the tribe may have been:

"Welcome, welcome, welcome,

To you, the unique one,

Of creation.

May you know yourself,

As you walk the great earth

With the song of the Sidhe in your heart,

And joy leaping like a deer from your eyes."

The chants continued thus, for one hour non-stop, whilst each person held the child warmly to their hearts and gave her/him their heart gift. Whilst the child was cradled by loving others, the mother was then given the blessings of the grandmothers. This was in the form of a chant started by the oldest grandmother and taken up by the others, in turn:

"Oh! Holy one,

Mother creator with the Goddess,

In the earth of you new life came through.

How can we serve such a one?

How can we be your helpers?"

The Fifth *Áite* of Birth
The Afterbirth or "Shawl of Goddess"

The youngest mother helped the mother to expel the placenta from her womb by means of oils, massage and sound. They wrapped the child in it warmly and placed her/him on the mother's breast. This time of togetherness was for mother and child alone. Later the mother either ate the placenta herself or put it in the earth. The eating of it ensured that no disease would come to the mother and subsequently to the child. The place where the placenta was buried was called "Place of Treasure". It was said that whenever the child needed a reminder of her/his importance in the community or if he/she got sad, they could go to the "Place of Treasure" and know they were welcome in that community, and were an important member of it. (When a person died, their remains were also put into this place in the earth where the shawl was buried. "Into the birthing place of all we gently lay your red blood shawl.")

As above so below; as there is a stage or *Áite* of review after a person dies, there is likewise a place of preview when the soul comes to earth. We are taught that this stage can take place between birth and the third trimester, when the soul previews her/his life and perhaps gets scared of the many lessons ahead. Sometimes a soul may go back to the spirit world and come at a time more appropriate to its stage of learning. This is the soul's decision.

The *Áite* of Death

As with birth, we experience the different stages of the *Áite* of Death chronologically from the first (peaceful transition or confusion) through to the fifth (marriage of soul and spirit or place of darkness).

After-Death Journey of Those Who Have Integrated Earth-Mind and Soul

1. Peaceful transition (Shape-changing) from body life to spirit life. We experience total relaxation and letting go of the past life. We hear the call to leave the clay body and we do so with total surrendering. We delight in the lightness of the new energy. We are able to let go totally of dense matter because we had learned firstly to live fully on earth and then detach fully before our transition. There is no place for fear to enter as we had made friends with all the unacceptable components of our personalities and those of others. We have returned all to love's healing power. Spirit beings greet us with warm welcoming. Our own projected love awaits us. The transcended love of those whom we loved in body will also be there to welcome us at death. Our minds will be able to produce whatever we desire, as we will have left the limitations of the earth body behind. (e.g., if we desire to see a mountain or tree, or a dead relative, we just have to visualize this and it materializes.)

The relevance of the first Áite for us whilst still in body

It is important to realize that according to the "Teachings from the Cauldron" we do not go "out there" to a place of light but deeper into the light and love of our own enlightenment. It is also important to do much visualizing work before we let our bodies go as this seemingly facilitates clearer vision after death. It is advisable to get used to ecstasy! Our consciousness needs to expand, for that is the essence of consciousness—what it is meant to do. The more joy we can experience now, the more we can project it in the world of spirit. The more we can let love guide us here in earth, the more we can be led to a place of real joy in our spirits later.

How easy is it for you to let go of situations? Are you stuck in the past and unable to adapt to little transformations? Now is the time to live in the moment so that when death comes it will simply be "the next moment".

2. Place of tranquility (Summerlands) where we experience bliss and total joy. This is enhanced by a waterfall of sounds, which vibrates as music and colour. This sound is called the "Breath of the Goddess/Gods", or blessed ones who have a particular interest in the evolution of earthlings. Some people are visited by their loving, encouraging energy at this time in our human development. They bring the energy of mercy and self-love. From a place of compassion we take a look at the earth plane which we have left behind and we are shown the good energy we have created there for the benefit of others. This harmonic resonance begins to build up the more people are willing to share love and joy on earth.

Relevance of the second Áite for us whilst still in body

To be able to appreciate what life teaches us in the form of beauty, colour and sound is an important preparation for this stage of our death journey. Remembering the connectedness of all nature enhances our ability to embrace bliss and harmony in this life and in the next. To live love and share our gifts unconditionally helps towards the spiritual evolution of our planet. May the world be a richer place because we have been here.

3. Review of life (listening to the stories): Our own guides will be present with us and, in a place of compassion and lightness, we listen to and see with the inner eye, the "story" (life) just lived and all other stories that went before. A non-judgmental appraisal of our lives will take place, in an attitude of self-forgiveness. If there is unfinished business, it can be done in a place of humility and gratitude. We see our past "mist-aches" in terms of not having seen the whole picture clearly; we "ached in the mist of not seeing clearly". We feel truly satisfied with our life experiences, if we have truly tried to live from the heart of creation.

Relevance of the third Áite for us whilst still in body

Sometimes it is a good practice before going to bed to make an appraisal of the day. This is not a time of self-judgment or self-criticism but a reflective moment of revisiting our actions of the day in an atmosphere of peace and forgiveness. We may decide to change some of our attitudes and let love flow through us more and, if there is someone for whom we held a grudge, we can send them rest and inner peace and decide that should we be granted the grace to live until morning we may have a chance to speak with them still.

4. Place of projection (*Tir-na-Sorcha*): If I do not judge my life from a place of guilt or despondency, but lovingly see it from the perspective of a mother/father when they ask a child to look at why they did a misdeed, I will enjoy a projected place of light, and be able to see through the eyes of love rather than through the voice of condemnation. No one else sits in judgment of us. There is no God on a throne to condemn us to hell or bring us to heaven. As I perceive myself to be, so I am. I see my own light shine on me and I will be able truly to experience unconditional, therefore unemotional, love and in this place of total acceptance of my soul I will be able to project a place of kindness, true peace and unlimited delight for my spirit.

Relevance of the fourth Áite for us whilst still in body

Self-compassion is the beginning of healing for if I hold a grudge against myself I am not in a place of joy or love. This, in my opinion, is the sin against the Holy Ghost that is referred to in the Christian catechism. It is the arrogance of the earth-mind that judges the soul and will not give it peace. "As above, so below" is a relevant adage; when I look inside with the eyes of love, I can look out and see only love.

5. Marriage of soul and spirit (Union of day and night, dark and light): This is the place of consciousness where the soul and spirit enjoy their union, the holy wedding, the merging with the light of our own love, our own divine natures. The law of love demands that all come together in love in the end and all worlds have to unite. This is the law of balance and equilibrium. The power of unattached and unemotional love has to become a reality if the human race is to reach its potential of greatness and peace. Each soul influences the next generation and so this responsibility is on everyone's shoulders, so to speak. Brigit said, "Breathe together and let the gift of breath bless the one giving and the one receiving, for in the end there is only receiving." In this way, i.e., living love, souls are better prepared to face the great work ahead of them as they enter into earthliness again. I may choose to remain in this place of joy or go to the rescue of other souls coming home. I may also decide to incarnate for the sake of others still in darkness. From a place of wisdom I will know what is best for all. Souls who go out again from a place of love and service are called *Solasú*; they are the caregivers and bring light and love. If a group decide to go together to help humanity they are named *AnamA-le-céile*.

An old *Seábhean* called Biddy McGill, used to speak of "the many rooms in Heaven, big enough to house the whole of the world and more". She often added, "And I hope I don't get myself lost and me on my way to see himself." Meaning, she was hoping to meet up with her husband again!

Relevance of the fifth Áite for us whilst still in body

When I have reached a place of joy in my own life, when I have integrated the shadow, I can then be of better service to another. Often one will experience the delight of meeting up again with other souls who decided to come into bodies to help others. It is as if we have known each other for ages and yet have just said "hello" this time. These *AnimA-le-céile*, or light- and care-bringers, while still needing to evolve more spiritually, could have chosen to do so in spirit. Out of compassion for others, however, they contracted to come into bodily form and help in the harvesting of love.

After-Death Journeys of Those Led by the Earth-Mind

1. Confusion (House of Donn, the dark God): Questions such as: Where am I? Am I dead or alive? What has happened to my body? disquieten many newly disembodied beings. This sudden "shape-changing" leaves the ego-mind very annoyed and full of anger. The House of Donn in Celtic folklore was a place of great darkness and oppression and one could not escape it. If one has identified oneself only with material matter, one will be in shock for some time after death as they will not have material things around them. People, who identified only with bodily life, roam around the spirit world looking for their bodies; they cannot let go. They often try to re-enter the body sometime after death. (They try to return to their former shape.) They may remain Earth-bound. Prayers are very necessary for such souls.

Relevance of the first Áite for us whilst still in body

If I believe that my identity is with physical matter only, that there is only void after life on earth, I make bold to say that I will be greatly surprised. Energy does not die, according to science, so the energy that was/is me, i.e., my soul, will transcend material form. It would seem to be a good suggestion to practise a form of meditation and get in touch with our own divinity before leaving earth life. For many, the word "spirituality" is meaningless and they live only for self-interest and self-gain, to which end they will shoot and kill and terrorize. This is not a judgment; this is just the way it is, and for this incarnation this is how they perceive life. This will change as they progress on the journey to self-liberation and each incarnation will facilitate this liberation. It is not for us to judge but to see how easy it is for us to deny our divine natures and live from our earth-mind only. As they are, so we were, so there is no room for judgment, only compassion and deep mercy.

2. Place of remorse and regret (Place where the Morrigan, the Goddess of shape-changing, meets the soul in the form of a screaming hag): It is the dark hovel of our own unhealed demons of sexual misconduct, lust, unmet and unholy desires, murderous intents, violent outrages against another so as to harm them, annihilation of that which is innocent and good. There is loss of integrity culminating in self-hatred because of paths not taken. Memory of having abused haunts us, as does our interrogation and manipulation of others. Our own demons of greed and envy devour our soul. It is the state of consciousness where ego-mind tries to get rid of the soul yet cannot kill it off because it is indestructible. This is a place of deep hatred for self and all created phenomena, a battlefield where the polarization of light and dark exists.

Relevance of the second Áite for us whilst still in body

To live with remorse and guilt is to live in a kind of self-made hell. When we lose integrity and self-honour we lose our souls. How do you lose your integrity? In what ways do you sell your soul? Do you ever ask forgiveness for having harmed another? Are you living your life with honour? Now is the time to seek harmony with yourself and the world.

3. Review (Place of stories): After some "time" of adjusting to the shape-change and realizing the unconsciousness of the life just lived, guides help these souls to adapt to their immaterial world. Help is always near but our souls have to ask for and see the need for help. We cannot change alone, pain, remorse, guilt and self-loathing fill us and we judge our life review without much mercy. If we hurt others intentionally, our souls show the suffering and we will experience it. The guides, however, love unconditionally, and help is there for us if we desire to change. This can take a long time, but time is of no consequence to soul.

Relevance of the third Áite for us whilst still in body

Are you able to accept help when offered or are you too stubborn or proud to accept it? It is a healthy reminder to us that as we give, so we shall receive. If I spend a lifetime hurting others or undermining them then, somehow, the universal law of "what goes around comes around" applies.

4. Place of projection (place where dragons fight in the form of animals as in the story *Mabinogion*): Our own judgments of ourselves send us to a place of fear and dread, i.e., hell. Sometimes poor souls have a need to return to Earth, as it is all they know. They are attached to the earth plane and cannot adjust to being without the density of a body.

They often in-body too quickly, before any lessons have been learned, and the consequences can be quite devastating for them. Many times, alcoholics who die in a drunken state return to haunt bars and lounges and literally hang on to the people there. As alcohol makes the astral body more accessible, they often enter into such a body, encouraging the person to take drink. Alcoholic ancestors, who have died whilst drunk, often possess the bodies of relatives and such people cannot give up the drinking habit.

This is a place of wandering and wandering alone with deep self-dejection and abandonment with no redress. It is the place of fire and burning that does not cease since their passions and greed create the fire. Faces of people they had tortured or abused comes to haunt them. Usually they do not ask for or accept any help given to them as this is out of character for them. Prayers are necessary for the souls of terrorists, as their own arrogance may not allow them to ask for help or accept it.

Relevance of the fourth Áite for us whilst still in body

It seems futile to repeat here the importance of integration of past regrets so that we can project a more peaceful and fulfilling life for ourselves. I will however state that according to the "Teachings from the Cauldron", such information is crucial to our peace of mind in this dimension and the next. We can daily remember the dead and especially the people who died creating acts of violence and murder.

5. Place of great darkness (*Áit an dorcas mór*): The light of the helping spirits around them scares the suffering souls, as they are so bright. The thought of going to the light frightens them more as they slowly become aware of their own state of hell. They themselves realize that they are not ready to unite with spirit and so they stay in despair. Many just fall into tumultuous sleep for a time. I was shown this to be a place of stupor and sick dizziness. Prayers and incantations are necessary for the release of these souls from the torment of their own egos. Instead of descending into this violently sick stupor, others have a deep impatience to "in-body" (embody) and some do so to their horror; the life they are about to embark on is not any happier than the previous one. This time they will experience the kind of pain they inflicted on others, as they did not integrate it all in the place of review. This means that they had no sorrow for their misdeeds. If they had not learnt from past mistakes and were impatient to reincarnate, they carry this impatience with them to the earth plane.

Relevance of the fifth Áite for us whilst still in body

Ignorance is the sleep of the unconscious. It is the place of forgetfulness, where we have forgotten our birthright, our divinity. Patience with our own ignorance, though, is essential to healing. There is a time for all things and our willingness to awaken is all-important. We must be gentle with our dear earth-minds and not condemn them for their place of not knowing. This patience will help to uncover the pearl of great price within us. It is important to remark that the Cauldron teaches that, when a person dies in a car accident or the like, and has had insufficient time to prepare for a so-called happy death, it depends on how easily they can adapt to change as to whether they bypass the place of confusion or remain there for a time, whilst they adjust to the new surroundings.

When someone dies by taking their own life before the allotted time, or before they had contracted to die, they usually go to the projected place of hopelessness in which they died. Always remember that such souls are helped to recover, are given all compassion, and love. Many regret having taken their lives and they are able to receive love. Some remain earth-bound and attach themselves to earth for the time they had "planned" to be here. This is a place of no-man's-land for them, very isolating and despairing all over again. Suicide is self (soul)-destructive and self (soul)-abusive. It is an attempt to kill the soul by the ego-mind and does not end with dying. We need to send our unconditional love and great support to people who have taken their own lives, as it is an arduous journey from self-hatred to self-acceptance. Children who die always go straight to the place of unconditional love and joy. Their earth-minds did not have control over their souls so integration is unnecessary for them. It is very disturbing for the various elements when one dies suddenly, it creates confusion and the shattering of the elements that constituted form is very traumatic. The same happens in the death of someone who is shot – sudden death is not an easy passage for soul.

May we all learn to love ourselves and thus all created phenomena whilst still in body and create for ourselves a "Summerland" and a *Tir-na-nÓg* in this life and in the next... *Seá* ("Amen").

PART TWO

Dealing with Your Personal Death and Dying Process

Natural Transformation as Death Approaches

It would take quite a few volumes to try and fully comprehend the vast transformations that take place in the body mind as death approaches. I will attempt, in a simplistic way, to state the general transformations which take place, as I was shown them in a place of meditation.

Allegedly, 28 days before death happens, the soul starts preparing herself for the journey. In the case of the terminally-ill person, the soul begins to withdraw slowly from earth life. This is natural and helpful both to the dying person and relatives. The former is given time to complete earth business whilst the latter has time to adjust to the final parting of their loved one. Clearly, all energies—physical, mental, emotional—are dedicated to the work in hand, i.e., the letting go of incarnation and concentrating on excarnating, the widening of soul into spirit. The dear body has almost ceased to function. It tries to contain consciousness and cannot do so. The unworked-through emotions still held in the body—the held-in hate, the remorse, revenges, the things we could have done and the things we should not have done—may demand release.

Whilst the tired physical body may persist for some time, there is little consciousness left. A simple way to understand the systems of withdrawal according to the "Teachings from the Cauldron" might be as follows: It teaches that the elements leave the material body in the order they entered at birth. At birth, however, they undergo cathexis and bond with soul whereas at death they undergo de-cathexis. (Tibetan Buddhism, however, teaches that water is the second element to leave the body at death.)

Earth body releases	Body begins to dissolve
Etheric or second body releases	Fire begins to cool
Emotional body releases	Water begins to dry up
Mental body releases	Air begins to leave

When the **Earth** begins to leave, and this can take quite some time, (it actually begins years before) one may notice the following changes in the person: The body itself will have little or no energy with which to do anything. The head will be as heavy as that of a newborn child with little or no self-direction.

The dying person is totally dependent on help from others to bring ease or physical comfort. The body may twitch as if in pain but, at this stage, it is the body's involuntary reflexes one sees. Often the dying person may ask to have the blankets removed, as their weight feels too heavy on their legs. At this stage one may help by assuring the dying person that all is well, that everything is happening as it must and the body can just relax into the earth. If they are in bed, remove any clothing that appears to be heavy and assure the dying person that they are not alone.

When the **Fire** begins to leave, the following may be noticed: The dying person may appear annoyed and anxious. The heat is leaving from the feet up and the temperature fluctuates. They appear to be frightened and at this stage one may experience the fires of so-called hell. It is as if one is being consumed by a great flame. The passion for life is now ebbing away and the voice also leaves. There is no muscle control.

At this stage, again, reassure the dying person that they can just release any tendencies to blame or to be consumed with anger. Assure them that love is all that is left now, only love. This is the stage where I share again with the dying people their own story and I always add that they did the best they could with the knowledge they had at the time . . . that all is forgiven, etc. They sometimes see the body or image of a loved one or someone they need to forgive. The words "all is forgiven" are important at this stage. Say the words into their left ear, as this is the ear of inner listening.

As **Water** evaporates, one may notice the eyes drying up and the mouth and nose are no longer moist. Sight can no longer differentiate between objects and smell has left. The blood congeals and the complexion is white and clammy. The legs begin to get very cold. Often a gurgling sound is heard from the throat and, as the throat muscles are no longer working, there may be white foam from the lungs coming from the mouth.

Again, remind the dying person of the journey ahead, that the ocean of joy and love awaits them. The internal sensation may be one of drowning in water and they cannot swim. Assure them that they are safe, that they do not need the breath in order to be alive and that only love surrounds them now.

The last element to leave consciousness is Air.

As the **Air** leaves, the breathing becomes very erratic. Often the dying person will appear to be dead as the breath only comes in small gulps. Then suddenly another breath comes and they begin to breathe again in a shallow way. This may last for a long time and one may wonder why it takes so long for the breath to leave. The earth, fire, and water cannot hold consciousness now and the great wind is about to leave. Often one takes three breaths and after the last one, there are no more in-breaths; the soul has left the body. The elements can no longer hold the life force so it leaves to travel to spirit.

Now soul can concentrate on listening for the echo of its own voice calling itself inwards, calling it home, unfettered by material distractions. This voice sound, or *guth an anam* in the Gaelic, comes at birth and stays lodged in the nervous system in the form of a logos or word. During life, this call can be activated by great moments of bliss and out-of-body experiences. The Cain, which represents the ethereal nervous system, responds to the call and is attracted to it. This sound is heard as music, most sweet to the person who dies consciously and with love in their hearts. It is "that sweet love call" we heard about before. According to the Teachings, "soft be the sounds and sweet as honeysuckle the music heard by the soul released from earth in joy". At this stage, a profoundly deep vibration affects the Cain and the shadow body detaches. This vibration is the loosening of the *Corda Geal* from the energy spirals, starting with the lower ones. Many magnificent colours and hues flood the consciousness of the dying person and often this is made obvious by the serene look on the face. These colours all merge into one at the crown of the head and produce the illuminative white light. As the terracotta, orange, yellow, green-turquoise, indigo, and magenta all spiral up the body, the dying person experiences a type of dizziness as if tunnelling or spiralling upwards. A poem I wrote after my near-death experience in 1973 explains this phenomenon:

"I danced to rhythms of a song I knew

But never heard before

And with this new beautiful body

I became a harp for God's fingers to play on."

May the love of life help us to firmly establish ourselves here and may the love of our souls help us to fully experience de-cathexis from this life in order to live fully in the next.

The Paths Home

Most so-called experts on the dying process suggest that the life force or soul leaves from three different exits in the body, i.e., the solar plexus, the heart, and the crown of the head.

If one has tried to live a good enough life and has shared love with others, s/he will exit from the heart centre. The difficulty would seem to be that the emotional energy takes a while to clear from the heart and the letting go takes longer.

According to Celtic spirituality, we have many chances to reincarnate in one lifetime on earth. When we exchange the personal, emotional heart for the widened, universal heart, we see from the eyes of unconditional love and in our process of leaving the earth we go immediately to what has been termed "the bright light" through the crown of the head. This means that the earth-mind has been integrated into the heart of love and is no longer in opposition to the ways of spirit.

If we have hurt and victimized others, our soul will exit from the solar plexus, which still holds fear and terror. We take these energies with us as we journey onwards. If we have identified ourselves only with bodily life, we will find it difficult to leave the known and take that leap of faith towards the unknown; we will leave from the solar plexus. The earth-mind is still not integrated and it projects itself into the next state of consciousness.

Our journey is to become more and more closely identified with our soul's energy and live from its essence, as we will be attracted by the light of our own soul and we will go in the direction of spirit. This is the place of bliss and joy. Depending on the last thoughts in the mind of a person, s/he will go on to experience bliss, confusion, or fear. As thoughts determine our actions whilst in a body, they also determine the future of the soul as our soul does not interfere with our free will.

Naturally, there will be helpers in spirit dimension to come to the aid of people dying in confusion or stress, but they cannot interfere in our own process. If help is refused, there is nothing they can do. Here again the *Anam-Áire* can be of great assistance to the passing soul. S/he can help change the energies from fear to love, if the dying person wills it. If not, then s/he may continue to pray for the continuous release of the soul from a place of stuckness to a place of freedom in itself. Here is an old Irish prayer:

"Oh, love that spills
Into all the worlds of seen and unseen,
Stay with me in those last breaths,
Brigit, blow a kiss to my hard heart
And soften it with your lullaby."

The Celts were very involved with death rites of passage and the care of the soul in the after-life of *Tir-na-nÓg* or *Tir na Sorcha*, land of light. The *Anam-Áire* was an important helpmate to the dying during, and especially after, death and followed them to the last *Áite* in the next world, suggesting different routes to follow in order to reach their soul's resting place (I will enlarge on this subject later in the book). They introduced an order called *Ceile De* ("with God"), which reminded people to pray for the dead. The Catholic Church follows this practice of interceding for the dying, and prayers and intercessions for the souls of those who have no one to pray for them is still practised by many. The Celtic Christian Church offered various chants and Gutha mantras on behalf of the dead. One such mantra is the following:

"May God and his wife bless you
May Brigit and Michael bless you
As you go home.
May your Angel bless you
When your Devil comes from the fire
May your own clan be waiting for you
And you safe in the arms of Jesus."

It is interesting that one's own devil was referred to. It was accepted that one had a personal angel and devil. When one dies consciously, all the energies are directed towards the internal light of love. This is our deepest concentration. This is where all our attention is focused. We can also be conscious of being with our loved ones and give our attention to the dying adventure. Many times I have witnessed being with a dying person who suddenly looked into the eyes of their Beloved, smiled a gracious smile and then released their soul to spirit. Such treasured memories for all present. The one who has spent a lifetime giving care to their soul dies with the joy of one who has finished the course and now lays one's burden of earth body down to rest.

Slip Away

In the case of an underdeveloped spiritual persona, one whose earth or ego body is still in charge, the etheric body hovers around the room after the soul has left, as the leaving was so painful emotionally. Often there seems to me to be a battle going on between the soul and the etheric body, the one longing to leave and the other hanging on.

An indecisive person sometimes has such difficulties of decision-making. It is as if the will is not strong enough to make the decision. Such a person will often just hang on in there for a long time. The old ones used to say, "If you pray for his soul, he will leave through the mist at the top of the head. If you don't, then he will be hanging around the kitchen looking for food." Samhain was a time for praying for the dying and "speeding them away".

At the same time, we cannot and dare not come to any set conclusions as to the sacraments that take place in the soul of one making his journey out of bodily life. *The Dying Person alone knows the mystery they are experiencing.* Often, as in the case with my own father's death, it was not until the last weeks' that he was able to receive love and self-compassion. I am so grateful for those weeks which, if he had died sooner, we would not as a family have had the time to be with him, cradle him in our love and help him to open his heart to receive our love and gratitude. He had died as he had lived, taking the slow pace of the angler he was in his leisure hours, easing his way down the river, to where he knew he could find a place on the bank to sit and rest and be.

It is more painful, I am sure, for the dear ones who sit up month after month waiting for the dying person to show signs of heart failure so that they could leave soon. Often from a place of exhaustion, they will confide in me: "I wish they would go, it has been so long and so tiring just hanging on day by day." My song encourages the dying person to:

"Slip away, no need to fight,

Out of the shadows into the light,

Out of your body into a life

Where freedom calls you.

Go dear love
No need to stay
What's left undone
Is for another day
All pain is gone
The angels sing
And beauty calls you

I will miss
The times we knew
I'll cry my tears
And know that you
Will watch with me
When my time comes
And you will call me

May joy be with you
and may peace
draw the curtain that separates
your world from mine
till another time
when love will call us."

It is true that many people learn great and precious lessons during the last month or so of their bodily lives while consciousness still resides in the earth body. Others just find it difficult to depart even though the body is very ill and not truly functioning well. It is often a matter of staying with what we know instead of going on and entering the next phase of life. On the other hand, if there are things we have not accomplished whilst in earth, we will find it difficult to leave. If there are those to whom we need to say goodbye, we will wait until they come and then we can leave. The dying need also to complete, to finish the journey they began with people on earth especially family. So many things get in the way of our farewell. I have experienced people who have not lived their potential, staying around in a body hoping to accomplish a task of one kind or another before they go.

"I Have a Dream"

I witnessed a young woman who had always wanted to be an artist but instead she became a maths teacher. She was confined to bed as cancer had taken its toll on her life. She confided to me her disappointment with herself for not having followed her dream.

I borrowed a large box of paints, a brush and a large sheet of white cardboard paper, which I placed in front of her, leaning against the bed tray. The jam jar of water was beside her in a bedpan (you do what you have to do to be creative!). I found an old plastic bed sheet, placed it around the bedclothes, and put a plastic apron around her. She sat up in the bed, idly dipping into the paints and looking somewhere in the distance as if searching a scene in her mind's eye. I said to her, "Annie, close your eyes, see the most beautiful country scene (she loved the countryside and nature), see it very clearly, see every detail, be in it for some time, smell it, walk in it and when you are ready, still with your eyes closed, begin to colour this lovely scene. Do not worry about messing with the colours, all is perfect."

I put on the cassette tape of her favourite music and sat in the room beside the door, making sure no one entered whilst she was creating her dream. As she put the brush into the colours, her face simply glowed and her shaking hand filled the white cardboard with mountains and rivers, trees and birds. At the top left-hand corner a bright sun shone and when Annie signalled to me that she had completed her picture, I took it and the paints from the bed and she happily lay back on the pillow. Her work done, she was ready to go. The wonderful thing is that the scene stayed with her and I do believe without a doubt that she went directly there when she died during that night. The picture was a poignant reminder to her husband and family to live their lives from their hearts, not from the place of duty or "have to". Her husband changed his job the following year. He had been a bank manager: he is now running a restaurant in his home!

When Jesus the Christ hung on his cross, he said, "It is finished." These are very poignant words. In the old Gaelic tradition, we say, "Tá críoch leis" when we have worked at our unfinished business. It actually means "I have nothing left." I pray that, when I am on my deathbed ready for the big journey, I will be able to say, "Tá críoch leis."

The old ones used to say that, if we have a task to complete and have not done so before we die, we will keep returning to the body or the place in order to do the completion work. I believe there is a lot of truth in this. That is one of the reasons I remind us all to live our own dreams, not the dreams of our parents or tribe. Sometimes on our deathbeds, it is not the things we have done that cause us regret but that which we failed to accomplish. May we all be able to follow our soul's pathway in life, i.e., follow our heart's delight and be ready to leave it all gracefully and with joy in the end.

connect with your dreams

What are the ideas and dreams you are putting off until tomorrow or next year or, "I'll wait until I have more time"?

What calls your heart, right now, to complete or begin?

What joy are you curtailing in this moment because "others might think I am silly", etc.?

If what delights your heart feeds your soul (I really believe this to be true), then why are you starving your soul?

Is there someone you love and you have not told him or her? Do it now; do not wait until you are unable to speak.

Is there someone you hold outside your heart and with whom you will not speak?

Can you risk taking the step towards them today, even if you truly believe they are at fault?

Remember, what frees your heart feeds your soul.

After the Death of the Body

What I would like to explore are my subjective findings around the subject of life after death, which may help dispel some of the uncertainties around the ideas of purgatory, limbo, heaven and hell. Tibetan Buddhism teaches that there are five lower realms of existence to which one descends if one is not vigilant. These include hell beings, hungry ghosts, animals, titans, and humans. Seemingly, these realms are all contained in the state of sensuous desire and are not located in a particular place but exist within our own psyches.

This is very much in keeping with Celtic spirituality and philosophy. Again, it is about integrating the dark and the light. As children, we were warned that unless we were very good and obeyed the commandments of God, we would go to hell and burn in flames that "never go out and the devils put red hot pokers in your eyes continuously and you are thirsty all the time and have no water to quench it". This may be the state of mind of those who hated all their lives, or were on fire with envy and rage; these states survive bodily death. Many church teachings were a means of controlling the masses, with no respect for the individual's innate or acquired morality. The sad reality was that intelligent adults believed the same. It was as if personal morality were insufficient and that an imposition of such from the Church was necessary to ensure right conduct. This was the Christian doctrine taught in Ireland up until the 1980s. The irony was that alongside these teachings we were also taught that Jesus died for our sins so that we did not have to go to hell! This was such a confusing theology to accept, that someone should have died to prevent our being punished if we were going to be condemned anyway!

Now I clearly see it as a means of manipulation and a method by which the hierarchy kept a strict eye on the fearful faithful. From my personal interactions with Catholics, it would appear that this doctrine is, however, no longer accepted by the majority and seems to have been assigned to the archives under the heading "myths and mystified memorabilia". Whilst the idea of Jesus having died to set us free would seem to be myth rather than reality, the consciousness-states of heaven, hell, purgatory, and limbo do have a reality in both this world and the next. However, it is not about a God "up there" judging us continuously; it is rather our own ignorance and self-hatred that keeps us locked in the many states of torment and unlove, which we then project into the world.

Our ancestors have a chance to heal with us.

How Can We Live and Die Consciously?

Brigit's Cauldron (wisdom) teaches that:

- The most important death that takes place is the releasing of the earth-mind into the mind of love and this release must begin whilst in bodily life.

- The last thoughts that fill our minds as we die determine our consciousness after death.

- We ourselves project heaven or hell in this world and the next.

- Limbo is the place in life or in death wherein we stand at the threshold of change.

- Purgatory is what we experience in life and after-life when the dear earth-mind is still attached to regrets and remorse.

- We can at any time exchange a heart of stone for a heart of flesh.

- Our soul knows exactly what we need: our earth-mind only supposes.

- Human beings are the embodiment of the Divine.

- Each has his/her own journey to make.

- Getting clear of emotional dysfunction is spiritual work.

- Illness needs to be looked at from within a spiritual context.

- Conscious living is spiritual work.

- We are all interconnected; karma is redirected projections.

- The healer is within.

- The earth-mind must be healed into love.

- Conscious dying is now.

- All the worlds of creation are holy.

- Community is important; we do not heal in isolation.

May we all learn the lessons of love here and now in bodily form, as it is more difficult to learn the lessons after death when we are out of our earth bodies.

May we live our lives consciously, before we die.

May the love of life help us to earth ourselves firmly here. May our souls help us to undergo de-cathexis in order to live fully hereafter.

Some Lessons to Learn
While We Are Still in the Body

Remember, life is there for you to do what you will with it and sometimes it is our will that is weak and does not support our creativity. Therefore, creating a strong and supportive will or *animus* is important.

What do you need to change in your life?

Is there a possibility that you expect perfection from yourself? Listen to the inner voice; if it is always telling you that you are not good enough, then you need to change the tune and begin to create an inner voice of love and self-compassion. Remember that your soul will never condemn you; it is the voice of your judge that you are hearing. You alone can decide which inner voice you listen to.

- Go for your dreams—now!

- Know that what delights your heart, feeds your soul.

- Live life fully in love with all creation.

- Everything is our teacher.

- Share your sad and happy emotions.

- Be willing to have your heart widened into life; go beyond your fears.

- Risk living at the edge for a while. Be aware of what you do and do not do because of fear.

- Listen more with your inner ear.

- Let go of attachments to people and things.

- Meet with people that you have reactions to, because these are your teachers.

- Let nature be your mentor.

- Tell people whom you love that you love them.

- Learn to adapt to change without losing your centre.

- Follow your soul, not your conditioned mind.

- What does not serve you does not serve another.

- Practise being extravagant with your love; smile at flowers and old people.

- Take up a new hobby.

- Take yourself less seriously.

- Buy flowers for yourself and send them to yourself with love.

Celtic Festivals of Transformation

To facilitate going deeper into life, the Celts ask us to tune into the rhythms of nature. These rhythms are demonstrated in the flow of the seasons and these are celebrated with joy and honouring of the spirit that dwells in them individually. The eight important calendar celebrations, denoting the rise, the manifestation and the decline of the great sun gods which affect nature, were ritualized within the communities. These are:

New Year — 31st October
Winter Solstice — 21st December
Brigid's day — 2nd February
Spring Equinox — 21st March
Beltane (or Bealtine) — 1st May
Summer Solstice — 21st June
Harvest—31st July — 1st August
Autumn Equinox — 21st September

Clearly, the four seasons in nature also corresponded to one human lifecycle, that is:

Season	Rhythm in Nature	Rhythm in Humans
An Earrach—Spring	springing into life	our birth in the earth
An Samhraidi—Summer	blossoming into life	living fully in this life
An Fomhar—Autumn	letting-go of life	letting go of body life in this form
An Gei—Winter	shape-changing	death of bodily life

These changes in nature, which are organic, also manifest within the human being. Samhain was a time for shape-changing or releasing and I offer an example of a releasing ritual here.

Samhain

Samhain falls between 31st October and 1st November, the beginning of the Celtic New Year. It was a time of release, of starting over, and it was essential to consciously release the old year so that the new one could be really welcomed in. Rituals of releasing were celebrated and the *Meitheal* (Gaelic for "gathering") all joined in. The following is an example of the kind of ceremony which took place (I use the term "priestess" as in many Celtic ceremonies the priestess represented Goddess; this is the ceremony given to me to celebrate):

The priestess, along with the people, made a *Tine geal*, or bright fire. The women and maidens gathered the twigs and small sticks while the men gathered the large branches and upright poles. This gathering was in silence. The gathering done, the priestess cast a circle and any animals that wandered in were welcomed. She then called in the protection of the four directions and the elements, which represented them. With a clear voice, she invited north, which represented earth; south, which represented fire; east, which represented air; and west, which represented water.

With their contributions of twigs and wood full in their arms, young and old placed themselves around the neat, circular clump of flat stones on which the fire would burn. As far as possible they stood male next to female, so that the energy got distributed evenly. The priestess then sprinkled sage and sweet grasses on to the stones and laid the first twig in the centre. She then called on the women to come and continue circling the twigs around it. When the last woman had laid her twigs around the circle, the priestess then lit the twigs and small branches. The fire started and the flames grew high. At this stage she asked the men to come and place their offerings, vertically standing around the burning twigs (the belief being that it is the feminine who births the soul in the masculine. She is the fire in which he burns his unyielding parts). It was not about hierarchical superiority; rather the Celts believed that the feminine represented the soul of nature, and was not attached to gender. They then all held hands and chanted the fire song:

"We give thanks to the fire,

For the breath of life be in it,

We give thanks to the fire,

Thanks and praise."

Thanksgiving for all of nature's gifts was important to the Celtic people. Their belief was that when we are grateful, the Great Spirit of Creation fills us *Lán do grastái*, full of graces or gifts. The priestess asked:

"What be the burning you give to the flames?"

One by one, the people came forward, stood in front of the lit fire, spoke their name and offered their burning, for example:

"I, (naming themselves) amongst us, give the pain I suffered at the death of my child as burning to the fire."

Another might add:

"I, (name) amongst us, give the failing of my crops as burning to the fire."

In other words, they surrendered to the fire the heartache of the past year as a burning gift, a precious gift to the flames. The fire in turn would transform their gift into something that would benefit their lives. This was great alchemy; this was the forging into gold of the hard metals of their lives. This is what we do nowadays when we consciously release pain and invite the abundance of life to fill us. When the last person had surrendered their so-called gift to the fire, the priestess added:

"Oh! Great fire amongst us,

Clean out what is not for harvesting in us

And fill us with your passion."

This done, she invited the *Meitheal* to turn their backs to the fire and, facing outward, she instructed them to let go of the hands they were holding and raise them upwards and give praise to the great spirits, Sun, Moon and Stars. This done she prepared them for the mighty *Seá* (the equivalent of "Ho" or the Christian "Amen") as follows:

With great enthusiasm, each person present thought within their heart what it was that they wished for their lives for the coming year. Satisfied that they had time enough in which to do this, the priestess signalled to begin the acclamation. Everyone bent their right hand to the earth and, slowly bringing it towards them again whilst taking a sharp intake of breath, they raised it to the sky whilst loudly acclaiming *"Seá"*. The breath was held out for a few moments, for in that time it was said that the Great Spirit of Creation gathered in their wishes and set about granting them. Everyone then clapped and danced individually around the fire. The children amongst them separated from the adults, formed an inner circle, danced and sang around the fire until the oldest man present called on them to go home and prepare for the coming of the Souls.

(The above is a ritual to do with friends. Change whatever is not appropriate for the group.)

Samhain was a very important rhythm in the life of a Celt. It was believed that the spirits of the dead come back to visit at this time. This visit can be threefold: to clear an old debt, to give a blessing, or to ask for prayers for themselves or another that may have got distracted on their spirit-journey and needed to move onwards to their resting place. The prayers for the dead were in the form of incantations, such as:

"May the sun of the Summerlands bless you this day.

May your soul shine through Brigit's window

And may she herself gather in

The parts of you still

Wandering around your home."

It was said that if a person was cursed or a bad intention was directed at them, they would come back and ask that the person retract their curse. Often the priestess or *Seábhean* (old Crone or wise woman) would openly ask in a *Meitheal* if anyone had "planted a bad word in the ear" of a deceased person. If they had, she would instruct them to ask for forgiveness and send them a "good word" instead. The belief was that the dead person would be earthbound until the curse was lifted. As it was a custom to burn the bodies of the dead after five days, it was necessary that any unfinished business associated with the dead person be finished within this time span. Otherwise, the soul might stay around waiting for release.

This idea of asking for forgiveness (releasing the blame) and completing unfinished business is still very important if we are to live consciously. During my workshops on "Death—the Final Healing", we build the fire as they did long ago and, using a dead leaf or a pinecone to symbolize any dysfunctional feelings, we cast it to the flames. Feelings of guilt, shame or fear prevent us from living the abundance of life and the fire can transform these into healing gifts for our lives. For instance, you can submit to the flames any grudges you may still be holding. This not only releases the person towards whom you bear the grudge, but it also releases you from the side-effects of holding them. We sometimes forget that when we think badly of another, or will not forgive them the pain they caused, we are actually hurting ourselves as we carry the negative energy in our hearts.

Nowadays many people visit their psychotherapist to unburden their psychological shadows.

Death Is Simply the Next Step

The most important teaching for me is a daily remembrance that dying is a natural state of life. Every time I say goodbye to my friends and family it is a letting-go of them. It is a kind of mini-death. Every birthday is a letting-go of the years. Every time we change house or job it is a reminder of letting go of things to which we have attached ourselves. For many women, when they have a breast removed due to cancer or womb removed because of disease, it is a letting-go of the body parts, a farewell to a part of us that lived with us for a long time. Divorce is a form of dying, of saying goodbye to the dream of being together with someone happy forever. Brigit reminds me that:

> "Dying is not something you do once:
> it is the continuum in life,
> Of receiving a gift and letting it go."

> "When you control your tears of grief,
> joy cannot dance in your bones."

> "Grieving is something you do,
> not just something you feel."

If only we could hold life and all its gifts as lightly as if it were a beautiful butterfly needing freedom to expand and fly and look into the face of the sun. The Cauldron asks us to live life consciously and fully. Is this a contradiction? How may we live life fully and at the same time let it go, set it free within others and ourselves? This seems quite impossible! And yet, if we want to be consciously aware in our everyday living we need to let go of one experience in order to live another one fully. It seems that the great risk we take is to be deep in life, knowing that it is not permanent. People say, "Why bother?" as it sometimes feels like it is not worth the struggle. Some find it too painful and cannot risk being fully involved, so they opt out in many ways. Something I wrote some years ago regarding this kind of depression includes the following:

An immediate antidote for depression is to have a place, a safe temple, where with non-judgmental others, one can "out" the rage against the injustices and hopelessness one perceives in life, for under the layers of rage grief waits to tell her story, too.

Anger is a movement: depression has none; motion is needed for transformation, and it takes the hand of hopelessness and teaches it to dance.

Eventually, of course, one realizes that the real cure for depression is to choose to move into life. To live it all.

Knowing that, the breath longs for expansion, but one cannot know this whilst stasis fills the blood.

People commit suicide as the idea of movement in a world of pain and suffering does not make sense to them and the idea of scattering one's heart into everything and all is too scary and, at best, foolish. Nothing matters any more; inactive grief takes over in the form of despair and they hope that at last they will not have to put any energy into breathing. The life force itself is barely present; it is as if it has left already, and there is no longer any attraction, no incentive to stay imprisoned in a house of ghosts. Others contract an illness that leaves them immobile, so they have a reason for premature death. (Naturally I do not suggest that this is why all people are ill.) I contracted anorexia when I was a young woman. At that time I needed a guiding, understanding other to help me take responsibility for my own life instead of allowing the overpowering influence of my mother to rule me. I truly wanted to die as life held no joy or interest for me. It was a kind of slow suicide, as I had lost so much of my body to the illness, and I screamed inside with the pain of unexpressed feelings. No one can blame another for decisions they make about their lives, and sometimes they make internal contracts of which they themselves are unconscious. I have learnt that to live my life fully engaged with all I encounter, whether it is joy or sorrow, I need to be able to release and not cling to the happy times of the past or the negative imprints of past suffering. The words of the following song helped me to deal with releasing a relationship at a time when all I wanted to do was to hang on, even though my life energy was becoming depleted by doing so:

"Before you can love someone
You've got to be free to let them go.
Before they can tell you 'yes'
You've got to be willing to hear 'no'.
Before you can sing love's song
You've got to let the teardrops fall."

This is an example of what the Cauldron means by living fully and letting go. Some stay outside, looking in on life rather than being truly in it; they chose to be observers of life, what the Cauldron calls "dancing with one foot". They prefer to stay safe in the sidelines and not appear on the stage. Maybe they need a compassionate other to invite them into the circle. Maybe they cannot invite themselves in. And this is their story, their way of being in life as best they can this time. The Cauldron teaches that we cannot and should not judge another's journey, as it is not our business, and therefore we have no right to criticize or condemn another. It is our business to be in life in the way that our souls guide us. How do we know we are being fully in life?

contemplate your life

1. What are your dreams? Do you dare to live them?

2. What are you doing because of fear?

3. What are you not doing because of fear?

4. How would you describe your life today? Is it generally:

A	Fulfilling
B	Boring
C	Full of fear
D	Full of joy
E	Not the life I had planned
F	Just getting on with things but nothing great
G	Lonely

. . .

5. What can you change in your present life to move closer to living your dreams? Even small steps lead forward.

You could go on answering questions like this and would be amazed at your answers. However, the Cauldron advises that life presents you with everything you need to live fully and consciously and for some this is difficult to imagine. Depending on the choices we make, our lives will be fulfilling or not. You may say, "Well what about illness, surely I have no control over that?" Again, the subtle choices we make indeed affect our health, especially if you believe that illness starts in the conditioned mind. Often the soul will make very good use of an illness to get us back on the track of healing our lives. Many people have used illness as a means of changing their whole lifestyle for the good of their soul's healing and, as already hinted, some chose illness (albeit unconsciously) rather than truly be in life. If we can live our lives as consciously as possible, going beyond our fears, feeling all the feelings, working through the pain and experiencing our creativity and joy at a deep level, we can reach enlightenment or liberation before we die.

According to the Teachings, the more we are willing to be with the grief of our life, the more we can be with the joys. They advise us that:

> "True liberation is living without fear, and enlightenment
> is being able to see the shadows and bring them to
> the light of consciousness."

This is difficult for many to accept. We think we have to become monks or nuns and pray or meditate all day in a difficult body posture, or give up all and follow some guru if we are to be enlightened. The Cauldron advises us to bring our shadows into the open space of love, where all is accepted, all is looked at through the eyes of mercy and all is precious fertilizer for the garden of life. This way, joy and creativity dance the vital juices of inner strength and outer well-being.

Lessons in Tough Love

For many years I gave a workshop every year with a dear friend, also a priestess, called Barbara Vincent, in Newbold House in Forres, Scotland, titled *Death—the Final Healing*. This may seem like a contradiction in terms; how can death be healing? The bigger question, however, is what do we mean by healing? We are used to defining healing as recovering body wellness and forget that, if the conditioned mind has not changed its old, dysfunctional patterns, we cannot reach healing; we cannot fully recover. I have watched many people with terminal illnesses looking for cures and miracles to make their bodies well again as if the body alone were their true identity. Some of them have remissions only to be smitten with the same or another illness in a few years' time because they have not changed any of their thought patterns regarding themselves or others. Other people have recovered and have totally changed their lifestyle because they have altered the way they look at themselves and the world. This change involves transformation. This change is about dying to the old and living with new awareness. The Cauldron says:

"The dear, conditioned mind needs to experience many deaths
if it is to be born again into love."

It teaches that when we are singing in harmony with our soul's song, the physical life is full of energy and wellness. When we live from the source of this love, everything we touch lights up in consequence. When we deny its power in us, we struggle with the conditioned mind that is full of doubt and inertia. I am happy to say that I have witnessed miracles whilst watching with dying people. People who had previously been full of revenge and blaming had reached a place of letting go of it all as death, the "leveller", approached. They could see how their state of mind had truly made them ill in the first place, how they had not allowed the gift of love to penetrate the dark recesses of their poor minds. What a shame that they had to be near death before the message finally got through. Learning to receive love is not easy and sometimes we have to experience "tough" love, which I call the lessons we have to learn in life. Many who are experiencing the final release of life see the lessons that they still need to learn, and many stay that extra day or night in their physical bodies in order to do so.

Learning to Receive Love

I watched my own father learn the lesson of receiving love, letting love in, a short time before he died. All his life he gave what he possibly could and he asked for nothing in return. We, as children, felt there was nothing we could give him and at times we felt quite unimportant. Before he died, he was able to reach out to his family and we did all we could to ensure his physical and emotional comfort. He was able to embrace us as we held him and told him we loved him. His eyes lit up and it was clear that he acknowledged this by the smile on his face. This was not to say that we also shared with him the difficult times we had living with him as a father, but to be able to receive love and our care was the healing for him and naturally for us, his children. He died at home with all the family around him. It was different with my mother; she did not want any of us to assist her in any way. She even asked us not to visit her or see her dying. She died as she had lived, reclusive and in control. She loved us deeply but was unable to receive our love and care and she was uncomfortable with our tears. This was so difficult for us and sadly, unlike my father, she was unable to take the last challenge to receive love. She died alone in hospital. I hope she will be better able to receive love the next time she embodies.

The Cauldron talks of the ways in which death teaches us about life. If we have not learned to receive love, we cannot fully partake in the joy and the support around us. If we cannot give or share love, we cannot fully be in life. It seems that we cannot die well either. It involves the cycle of give and take. It is about balance and harmony. It is about releasing the need to be in control of everything; it is about letting go of fear, fear of losing our sense of who we are (as dictated by the conditioned mind), of not being in charge of things, of letting go. I saw how this was so difficult for our mother all her life and how she did not change at death. Her sense of self was defined by how much she could control her life and the lives of her children. Her pain was never actively witnessed and in the end her dear heart could no longer contain the unexpressed agonies. It was attacked from the inside with all the controlled emotions of grief (she died of a heart attack). God's will was her defence against having to look at the hurts and great sufferings in her life. For her, it seemed that death was not the final healing but the final assault. Now she enjoys clearer sight and all is well. It is a shame that many people have to wait until they are on their deathbeds before they let go of their control and find freedom. Can you imagine how much more fulfilling our lives would be if we could release our insecurities before death?

If we are the authors of our lives, are we also the authors of our death? The Celts believed that we are. They chose when to die and that was usually naturally, from old age. When the men went to battle, they often chose to die as warriors whilst others knew they would survive as it was not the "proper time" to die. Is it actually possible, then, to project a so-called "proper time" to die? Perhaps we can decide now, consciously, when death should come. The old ones used to meditate on a happy death for all the family, visualizing each one lying in their beds surrounded by good friends and with a smile on their face. The following might be a practice to do before falling asleep:

vISualIZe youR death

Become aware of your body and how it feels.

Give thanks for all that the day brought. Notice if there were situations which were difficult for you. Now let them go.

Imagine you might decide to die when you are a certain age: 90, say. See yourself the way you would like to be during your last days. What do you feel? Is there contentment in your heart?

Now picture that you have died and you are peaceful and in joy. Remember the Áite and visualize your soul delighting in spirit. Just rest in love and feel the arms of love all around you as you sleep.

Let love breathe you to sleep.

PART THREE

Helping a Dying Person and Their Relatives

How Can We Help a Dying Person Make a Happy Transition?

How can we as helpmates with the dying assist them to make a happy transition?

What can we do? All we can do really is to be present if they wish this and to be attentive to their needs. Whilst it is my work to be with the dying should they need me, I am very conscious that I am dispensable. No matter how helpful I think I may be spiritually, I cannot do their journey for them; this is the work of their soul. I have been with many dying people and I am always amazed at the ways they challenge me by their authenticity and clear vision. Somehow, I have to be more honest with my dealings, not just with the dying, but also with people in general. I need to be humble enough to allow them to lead me and not vice versa, to remember always that I am simply the servant. I cannot heal them nor can I save them; this is the work of their own soul. That journey began the day they came to earth and no one can dictate when it will end. The healing is an inside job. Though many people have deathbed salvations, I do believe that for most of us we die as we have lived, e.g., if I have always been an impatient and impetuous person during life, the chances are I will be the same when I am dying; I will not want to wait around. Having said this, of course, one can have a complete change of heart as death approaches, a real healing, and I have seen very angry people becoming docile and gentle in death. I have also, however, seen very loving people behaving in very demanding and angry ways. I believe that "what we do not look at in life, comes up at death for recognition".

My grandfather was also a poet and the words of one of his poems suggest just this:

> "Leave not till death the raging war,
>
> That hides inside for fear of day,
>
> But here and now in mortal flesh,
>
> Let battle be and start afresh,
>
> So kindliness can have her say."
>
> —Charles McGill, 1932

He was a man of great honour and honesty and said with as few words as possible what needed to be said. He died quietly just as he had lived.

It is always a joy being with someone who experiences a peaceful transition, with dignity and grace. The problem, however, is our definitions of these terms; that which would constitute a happy death for one person may be hell for another! I am remembering an old man who was dying, who did not want a priest near him and did not want to be anointed:

"Will you make sure that 'himself' does not get his hands on me as I am dying?" I assured him that, if I were around at that time, I would do all in my power to prevent such a happening. (We must not promise something if we may not be able to fulfil it.)

"I don't want any rosaries or anything like that," he reminded me, "I just want yourself to sing *Danny Boy* in Gaelic; that would be a wee bit of heaven for me."

I am happy to say he had his wish. The family, however, were not as happy as they wanted to give him the best they knew, which would have been a Requiem Mass and all the trimmings. They did not realize that the old man, their grandfather, had given up religion long ago and was more inclined to believe in the holiness of the earth than in worshipping in a church. He also requested that I put some earth and newly mown hay into the coffin with him, together with a photo of his dead wife inside his jacket pocket. This I did with a smile on my face as no one knew about it, and that was what he had requested. Therefore, happily there are dreams that can wait until our dying day!

As far as is possible, it is important that people get the chance to die in their own homes. Nowadays this is becoming more the reality for many. In the old days it was the norm; people died in their own bed, with the family around, the dog at the bottom of the bed, the rooster crowing in the backyard and good neighbours sitting in the kitchen, eating the thick mutton soup. Death was a part of life, part of the comings and goings of life and not hidden away in a hospital bed in the city. I have good and comical memories of deaths and funerals that took place in my part of the country in Donegal. Children were always present at the deathbed of a relative and were present at births. I have the story of a family whose children were in the bed with the mother as she birthed their new sister. Later on, these children had a respect for life, their own bodies, and for life in general. They were part of the miracle of new life coming to earth and were there to experience life leaving the earth. They seem to be able to accept that pain is part of life's journey and that it is temporary. It was clear to me as a child that, although some people were in pain they were not suffering. Suffering happens when we identify ourselves with the pain and we allow it to absorb us completely. When we see pain as an enemy, an enemy that robs us of joy, we then project suffering onto the pain and we are in a state of agitation. Somehow, when a woman was having a baby, pain was present but joy was also there; they experienced the pain as part of the joy. My old Nanny McDyre would have said, "The two's the one." Such wise knowing in the old ones. In the olden times, children were included in their family's business; they were not alienated when a new being joined them in birth or left the family in death. They were part of birthing and dying. I have very clear memories of wakes and funerals in Donegal and they have given me most of my schooling regarding the work I do around death and dying.

"I Am Afraid of Pain"

It is important for dying people and relatives of the dying to realize that when death is imminent, there is a substance, a natural endorphin emitted from the pineal gland via the bloodstream into the heart, which is a natural painkiller. It relaxes the heart and often, if the dying person has had too much pain relief, s/he goes unconscious at this stage. It is vital, of course; that one remains conscious and there is no excuse in these days for anyone dying in pain. Medical research into pain relief has brought much breakthrough in this field, for which we are very grateful. Physical pain relief is always being revised and each dying person can have pain relief administered in a way that suits their particular pain threshold. The old days, of with-holding an injection of relief until the allotted time, are gone and this is so comforting to know for both patient and relative. It is reassuring to know that the patient may give themselves pain relief as and when they need it, whilst they are still capable of doing so.

I teach a very simple and short pain relief meditation to the dying which is simply:

Going with the breath and with each in-breath feeling the words,
"Release and let go into the pain."

With the out-breath feeling the words,
"I offer you my compassion and love."

The repetition of these self-comforting words can mean a lot towards softening around the place of pain and helping it to be at ease within the body-mind. It is like comforting a child who is paining. After a while one may have pain in the body, but it does not have to be in the mind. And one need not suffer with it. It is also a good idea to get help to fill in a "Living Will", as this will help people caring for you when or if you become incapable of caring for yourself or incapable of stating your needs regarding resuscitation and medical assistance during your last days. You can clearly state how you want to be treated.

The Stages of Releasing into Healing

Sometimes the psychological pain can be just as difficult for the patient to deal with as the bodily pain. Elisabeth Kübler-Ross, in her teachings, talks about the five stages of grieving, which can also describe the five stages of dying or healing. I have added, on number six, as I find it an important stage of healing: the stage of finding our soul again, and reaching out into life afresh.

1	**Denial**	Not me, not now (not my child, job, friend etc.).
2	**Bargaining**	I will do such and such, if only things can stay as they are.
3	**Anger**	How dare God (you, it, the pain, them)! Why me? It is all the doctor's (God's, their, her, his, your) fault.
4	**Depression**	I have nothing left, no breath to live anymore; everything is just too much.
5	**Acceptance**	So it has happened; I cannot change it. This is the way it is.
6	**Surrender**	I surrender to life to love. I embrace my earth life. (When the relatives of the dying person are experiencing the surrender stage, they move into a fuller more expanded experience of life, the grieving done.)

During our lives, we have to deal with loss and separation and these so-called stages are not linear. One may start with denial, go on to depression and acceptance and, just as we think all is accepted, up crops depression or bargaining. I have noticed this in myself when I have been in deep grief over a relationship that has ended.

The **Denial** sets in with internal conversation such as, "This is not the end at all; this is just the relationship going through a bad time," even though everything in me knows it is over.

Then I can go to **Anger**: "How dare he (she, it, etc.) do this to me!"

Soon I am in, "I am better off without him (her, it, etc.); anyway, I deserve better."

The **Bargaining** stage could include, "I will be a better person. I will change and all will be well."

Soon **Depression** sets in: "I am feeling the heart pain and can do nothing about it, and I feel hopeless."

Maybe, I will experience more anger and bargaining before the stage of **Acceptance**: "This is the way it is and I am very sad and I guess my life can go on."

When I get to the place of **Surrendering into Life /Reaching Out,** the internal process is soulful and encouraging and I have learnt from my active grieving. The heart feels, "I can find love again, joy again, a new job, etc., and I give thanks for the opening of my heart."

I know then that healing has taken place and I can reach out more and more into the world. With the person dying, they eventually get to the place where peace and self-mercy flow in and they are in the moment with their dying. I often say to nurses and hospice workers, "If you have not been able to 'watch with' (be present to) your own grief and pain and taken compassion on your own vulnerability, you cannot be with the dying and their relatives."

Elisabeth Kübler-Ross, M.D. (who died on 24th August 2004), always emphasized that we are of no use to the dying or bereaved if we are trying to "fix" them or ourselves. So many of us have been care-takers of others instead of care-*givers*; we care-take in order to get recognition and/or acceptance, so our giving is conditional. When we care-give, we are giving from a clear perspective of not needing anything in return. For so many years I care-took many people, not realizing how much I needed them in my life. Having worked with Elisabeth and having gone through the "tumble dryer" (her own words for the training she gave us), I realized that the only way to heal our pain is to work through it and not just try to positively-think it. Our humanity is our greatest gift as, through and because of it, we can reach our soul's glory in this life and in the life of spirit.

No one has ever given me such strong lessons in life as the dying have. The Cauldron asks us to be watchful of our own feelings around the dying, watchful as to how we treat them differently because they are dying. I need to be aware of what my reaction is and what my response to them is. The Cauldron advises: "Know yourself and let your soul speak through you."

Oftentimes, the dying show me the parts of myself I would rather keep out of sight. They challenge my so-called safe boundaries. I cannot pretend feelings, I cannot escape feelings. Their heightened consciousness sees through my defences and it is impossible to play games. It is often too easy to see oneself as the so-called saviour/rescuer and treat the dying person as if they were invisible and so talk about them, not *to* them. It is important to speak directly to the dying person as long as they can communicate.

Many a dying person can appear to be very inconsistent in their behaviour; one day in good form, next day angry with everyone and everything. Naturally, we think it is something we have done. When I examine the situation, I usually see that it has nothing to do with me or other people. It is their frustration, not being able to do the things they could have done a few months previously; having to ask for everything, even for the bedpan, can be so irritating for a previously active man or woman. To have to spend all day in a wheelchair or in bed because their body can no longer carry them is so depressing for people who, though they are terminally ill and have no hope of recovery, are still active mentally and still involved with their environment and everything in it.

If you have worked on your own frustrations in your life, your own impatience, you will be better able to be with others living or dying. If you have compassion with your own irritations, you will have mercy on those around you. Naturally, this does not mean that you put up with abuse or indignities from others; it simply means that when we know our own limitations, we are more aware of the limitations of others. We are servants of the dying, not their slaves, and there is a vast difference. Sometimes I have given tough love. The following is an example:

Having spent all night with Janet, who had cancer, and knowing she was neither in pain nor in need of anything, I left her in the good and loving care of another "watcher" at 6am. I was five minutes in the rest room, preparing to have a good sleep, when someone knocked at the door. I loathed opening it but I did.

"Phyllida, Janet says she needs to talk to you."

"Do you know what it is about?"

"No."

"Ask her, and if it is important. If it is not, then deal with it, please; I am getting some sleep until 1pm. Let her know I will be there at 3pm."

It may seem quite unreasonable that I should have done such a thing and I knew by the watcher's face that she felt insecure. I knew Janet had other very good people coming to be with her, so I was fine with the arrangement. I had a good morning's rest and after a shower and lunch, I went to Janet.

When I came through the door, she started to complain of being cold and not comfortable in the bed. The watcher advised me that she had had a good sleep and had not complained until I came!

Sometimes we find that dying people become attached to one person being with them and this provides them with security. However, having many people share the watching is wonderful as it is a big drain on one person's energy. When we are dying, we revert to childhood physically, emotionally, and intellectually. We have to depend on others to meet our needs and this is not easy for many people. Janet's behaviour was typical of what I mean. If we did not have a good, close mother presence when we were children, we seem to feel insecure when we are ill. As a child, I used to fall quite often but I would have waited until my mother came and then cried! Her attention and love was what I needed and the fall provided that. Janet died two months after that episode and we were all with her in the end. She learnt to trust that whoever was there was the "right" person, a great healing for her and, naturally, for others. It is also important to realize that we are not indispensable and that the dying person has all the help they need from their own wonderful inner resources.

The Power of Music:
Medicine for the Heart

The Celtic psyche is very attracted to music and dance, to poetry and song. They are the many ways in which the soul manifests herself through the personality. Brigit said, "When you tell a story, the heart listens but when you sing a story, the soul dances."

At Irish wakes (watching with the dying), it was very important that the dead person was in the midst of the celebration of his/her death. Each person present told a story pertaining to the dead person and usually there was a creative person present who composed a song or a poem on the spot telling the good deeds he/she performed on earth. This Celtic custom, of telling the story of the person's life back to them as they were dying and after they had died, helped the dead person to accept that s/he lived and died. It also helped the mourners to remember happy times shared with their beloved, which they may have forgotten. Witnessing was all-important to our Celtic ancestors. They believed that the story (life), which is witnessed on earth, is indelibly written down in the book of Stories in the Upperworld. Thus, many exaggerations regarding the good deeds done by a person were told in song and rhythm at their waking.

Music for the dying is now an accepted spiritual help, e.g. through the Threshold Choir. I have often been asked to sing for the dying person, but it has always been a song which they had known previously. Pat was such a person. He was sixty-five years old, had been a farmer all his life, and seemingly had a singing voice that reached deep into the soil in the heart of his listeners. He had wished to become a singer in his youth but never got away from the farm. Having had multiple sclerosis and a stroke, he was confined to a wheelchair for the last ten years. A soft, gentle man he was, who spoke daily with the animals and fed every hungry cat for miles. Not being able to milk the cows, saw wood for the fire, go for a walk with his dog, talk with the other farmers about the price they got for pigs at the fair, left him depressed and frustrated with life. His wife told me that the fact that he could no longer sing was what pained him the most; though he never voiced this, she "felt it in (her) bones". He sank into a deep, reactive depression, so much so that he refused to take part in any more conversations and was angry with everyone. Even his dog stayed well away. I called to see Pat one day and, having first spoken to his wife on the phone, I knew what to expect. I was surprised that he agreed to see me but he had heard that I could speak Gaelic so he was probably curious. I greeted him in Gaelic and he just mumbled something back. I said I did not have a lot of time but was glad to see him. "Would you like a song, Pat?" I asked. "If you want to sing, go ahead," was the reply through his teeth. I intuitively began to sing *The Isle of Innisfree*. I was about to start the second verse, when he began to shake in the chair. His wife looked concerned but I assured her with a smile that all was well. I could see that he was just fine, no need to rescue him at all. Her moving beside him, I felt, would have distracted him from his own process and he would have "pulled himself together" for her sake. I continued the four verses and did not stop, even though the shaking continued and deep sobs wheezed from him. Apart from a few stifled sighs, his wife remained silent. When I had finished the song, all that I heard was the deep grief pouring out of the big man in the wheelchair. His wife was now crying, too. What a gift they had given each other, such courage, such love. What a relief, I thought. Moreover, a time of release for his wife, who had done all she could to pretend everything was "just fine". I beckoned to Mary to join Pat and I left them holding each other whilst love held them both.

My personal belief is that the song did what all the tablets and all "positive-thinking therapy" failed to do and that was to help him get in touch with his own soul's healing and help Mary to release her love and pain. I left a tape recorder with him so that he could listen to the few songs I had recorded for him in Gaelic. Mary told me that he began to talk later that evening about Innisfree and the memories it brought back to him. When I called again, he attempted a song with me. He knew the words better than I did and he rebuked me for not knowing them properly!

"You'll be annoying the heads off the angels, Pat, when you get to heaven; you'll be telling them they are not in tune," I smiled. He smiled back and said he would teach them *Innisfree*. If Mary had had her way, he would not have cried that evening nor would she. She said she so much wanted me to "shut up the singing and stop making us sad", she added, "but it was the best thing ever happened to us." I advised her to share with Pat some of the photos of their grandchildren and talk about the day they married. The feedback I got was that they not only had a "grand night looking at all the old snapshots, but we had a glass of whiskey each and toasted each other again!" Mary added mischievously. "If the doctor knew himself had the whiskey, he would not be too pleased but it did him the world of good, and he slept well."

Sometimes, the heart knows about medicines not known to doctors. Patrick died three weeks later from a heart attack and with the recording of *Innisfree* playing in the background.

The Work of an Anam-Áire

The word *Anam-Áire*, as stated before, is from the Gaelic words *Anam*, meaning soul, and *Áire*, meaning care. The *Anam-Áire* therefore takes care of the soul, her own and of others. "Taking care of" means "having a care for", or "watching with". I like to think that as a Celtic woman I do both. The idea of an *Anam-Áire* is Celtic in its origin. Brigid, the Celtic Christian saint, has/d a great care for souls living and dead, and it is not unreasonable to believe that this vocation was handed down to her from the goddess Dana, also named Brigit, as she guided the living and dead to a place of self-honouring and peace.

I remember as a child how the old woman, or *Seábhean*, in the village or community was always present at the bedside of the dying, murmuring strange things into their left ear and splattering holy water over them; all around the room, especially in the corners, at the door, and under the bed on which the dying person lay. When I enquired what she was doing, she said she was "chasing the Devil away". Many years later, when my father was dying, my aunt phoned the house and instructed my sister Bernie to "shake the holy water all around the room and out the window and especially shake it under your father's bed, as this is the time when the Great War is on."

When my sister asked for clarification, my aunt told her, "Sure isn't this the time the Devil will be trying to get his soul and God will be trying to save it?" It is clear to decipher where this philosophy had its origin; the Cauldron teaches that at the time of dying there is a struggle between the soul and the ego-mind. The soul wishes to be free from the bonds of earth life and the ego holds on to what it knows and for some it cannot surrender to the light of love.

Another instruction my sister received from my aunt was to be sure and put the rosary beads in his hands, "because the Devil will try and take him by the hands but he won't touch them if he (father) has the holy beads in them". Wonderful rich meanderings of Celtic Christian traditions; my aunt knew so many of them. She used to keep the Brigid's cross above the fireplace and, at the time of a funeral, she would place it on top of the coffin as it was lowered into the earth. When asked why she did so, she answered, "Because when the devils see the cross of Brigid, they will take to their heels and run."

If someone questioned how she knew this to be true, she would answer smartly, "It is not for us to know the workings of a mighty saint of heaven; you need to have faith and not be asking too many questions." In other words, she did not have the answers, but she knew the traditions and that was enough. In times of hardship, faith in the workings of the holy ones was what kept the Irish psyche so optimistic. When there was a problem in the household, my grandmother would often say, as indeed was reiterated by my mother, "You don't see it now, but the saints and angels are watching over it all and they know what's best for us." They had a deep and unfaltering belief in the other worlds all around us, and they seemed to be able to transform their everyday consciousness in order to visit them. As language from one state of awareness cannot comprehend another, it was difficult for them to translate their experiences into more rational meaning. The Gaelic tongue translated these experiences more coherently, usually through the medium of poetry, art, dance and song.

Moreover, the "men of the cloth", namely the priests, frowned upon this. In many ways, these women were *Anam-Áires*, as they had a true care for souls and showed it in the ways they knew best. The old ones knew intuitively that death was not the end. "They will have a long way to go before they get to the pearly gates," old Hannah Gribben would say, as she sat by the bedside of the dying and, with her eyes closed, she would drone her Gaelic words in the direction of the dying person. Every so often, she would make a movement with her hand as if to signal to them to go on, to keep going. A prayer explains this:

> "Be going, dear one, be going,
>
> Your work is done,
>
> Be going to Brigit's hearth,
>
> God is waiting for you."

This is a wonderful way of being with the dying; giving them permission to leave as no one holds them back. It takes a lot of unconditional love for a mother to be able to speak these words to a dying child, or a young husband to his wife as she dies beside him, especially if they have not had time to adjust to their dying.

The Service of a Traveller
with the Dead

The main difference between a watcher with the dying and an *Anam-Áire* is that the latter is initiated into the thirteenth *Áite* of death if this be necessary. The watchers have been taught to travel as far as the fifth *Áite*, as it is not part of our training as hospice workers to travel in the after-life with the dead person. It is, however, important that good generous people, who already do wonderful work with the dying, get help to learn about "watching" with the dying as far as the fifth *Áite*. This is the stage when the soul travels on into unconditional love. I will show in the following chapter how watching may be done. The dead will travel through the mists of their own unfinished business from this incarnation and we try to be consciously aware of the difficulties they encounter along the way.

This service requires the most sensitive, unobtrusive involvement. Mostly we wait and watch with the soul in a space of altered consciousness, prayerful awareness of the work to hand, and detachment from the world outside the room and from any attachment to the dying person. A watcher may be male or female. It is mainly women who offer this service, but I am delighted at the many men who have shown an interest.

It is not our work to interfere in any way with the chosen destiny of the dead person, but to lovingly assist them, should they need assistance along the way—e.g., a person who has been mostly ego-driven in life will not be able (without great help) to let go into surrendering the ego to soul. S/he may feel frightened to let go finally into dying and be without oxygen. Can you imagine swimming and feeling panicky because your breath gets stifled? Another example might be if you are in a lift going upwards, when you may feel you do not have enough oxygen to keep you going and so you panic. People also panic when they feel they are alone in a house at night. In all panic situations, whatever they may be, the breath is affected. We need air and breath to remain in the world of matter.

When we are dying, we also have to get used to letting go of the breath. It is our link with both this world and the next; every in-breath is an "in-aspiration" to life, a calling in of spirit, and every out-breath is an "ex-spiration", a calling out of spirit. I recall my friend Sarah saying to me two days before she died, "Phyllida, I need you to tell me it is all right to let go of the breath; I seem to struggle with it."

This is exactly what I mean. We struggle to hold on and, in the dying situation, we need assurance that where we are going we do not need oxygen. My friend, who died some years ago, was also worried some weeks before her death about breathing. Consciously, she asked me to be with her in the last hours and to say into her ear, "Jane, let go of the breath; it is safe and you do not have to try to keep breathing in. Let go of the breath."

The fact that we say it repeatedly, the same words without changing either the rhythm with which we say them or the words we use, is *all-important*. Somehow it becomes a very sacred mantra, a mantra to help the personality let go and let the soul take over.

We always remember that the dying person is expanding their awareness of things around them more and more and is consequently susceptible to all that we hold in our minds. They see further than the physical eye and those who have been conscious of their dying process are very sensitive to the minds of the carers. It is therefore of utmost importance that the people with the dying are not at all afraid or feel insecure about what is happening and are able to send out clear and vivid messages to the dying without any feelings of fear, discomfort or any connectedness to their personalities. We do it from a place of loving detachment. It is important that the watcher lets the family know that their service is concerned with being with the dying person and does not involve the administrative side—such as organizing undertakers, the funeral parlour if one is requested, burial site/cremation centre, death registration, etc.

You as a watcher will, however, note the time of death if you are present at the last breath. If, however, you decide that there will be two watchers, one of you can help with information regarding all the administrative details before the death happens, so that you have this information to hand and need simply to supply it at the appropriate time.

It is of utmost importance that you get to know the person who has reached the stage where they have accepted that their illness is terminal and that they will die. I find that I always come to a patient by invitation only. For me this is important, as I do not want to appear as if I am evangelizing! Nor do I wish to give the appearance of offering a "How to die happy in three easy steps, by Phyllida, who knows it all" programme. Your first visit at their request will be mostly that of listening to them. Later, let them know the type of service you offer, i.e., that you are a "watcher" with people as they near the end of their life journey and only give information when the patient is able to sit up and take part in the discussion. Always let people know that you do not know everything about the dying process, even if you have been a hospice worker for many years. We are all students of the dying person; they are our teachers and we must not forget this. No two births are the same, no two deaths are the same so humility and unconditional love must attend us at all times. You cannot have all the information you need and often you have to use your intuition. No living person has all that information. We simply follow that which we have received from a greater wisdom, which grace has allowed us the honour of accessing at times when we need it.

Some dying people want to know everything regarding the dying process while others will not want to know anything. Some people are curious and just want to have a choice as to how and where they can die. Your caring for them is unconditional. This is their death and they need to do it their way.

Conscious living/conscious dying has not always been an important title for conferences or seminars. In the past ten years, however, I have been work-ing mainly with this subject. Nowadays we have the choice to live and die consciously if we so wish. There is no judgment either way. It is rather like when people are going to have an operation; some want to be told all about what the surgeon will do (and even then things happen differently from what is expected), while others do not want to know anything, but just to get on with it. A dear friend of mine called Eve wants her death to be filmed. This may seem macabre to many people, but she wants others to benefit in as many ways as possible by her dying. She has asked me to be there and watch with her as an *Anam-Áire* and I am happy to have said "yes" to this request. She is now dying consciously every day and is watchful of the changes tak-ing place in her body and soul. We keep in touch by letter and phone calls. She is a truly remarkable woman, over eighty years old. Another friend, also consciously dying, says that whilst his body is weak and without energy, his soul is soaring with joy and surrender. Another person dying at this time is consciously going through the different stages and, as the fire element leaves, her watcher tells me that she is doing great releasing of her fears and held-in anger. This encourages me in my life and work.

Some Important Things to Remember

- Ask the dying person whether or not they wish to be resuscitated when the heart fails to maintain their physical structure. If the person dying has filled in the "living will" form, the medical team will honour the state-ments made therein.

- Know the dying person's beliefs about their dying process and listen with lightness.

- Know their spiritual needs, if any. Do not impose yours.

- Gently find out any fears they may have regarding their death.

- Enquire respectfully if any relationship is not completed, i.e., if there is anyone needing their forgiveness, or vice versa. You can help them perform a little ritual of releasing. If they have a photograph it can be most helpful, as they can enter into dialogue with the person and release that way. Alternatively, you can facilitate a meeting with the significant other if both parties should require such.

- Know what they would like to have spoken into their ear by the watcher when death is imminent. Have a pencil and paper available and take down everything they say and read it back to them for verification.

- Find out if there is anyone in particular they would like to have in the room after they die.

- Let them know where your information comes from, i.e., what you believe happens at the hour of death when the breath is extinguished, and ask if they would like you to share it with them when they have come to accept that they are not going to get better.

Whilst the dying are still able to communicate, talk about the exact words you will be saying to them during the last stages of dying. If you need to change any wording, do it in their presence. They must have complete control over what is fed back to them. It has to fit their belief system.

Find out if they would like to have their family in the room as you do the watching with them. If they agree, then let the family also know what you will be doing. Suggest to the dying person that they can have members of the family say some of the prayers, chants or songs if they so wish. This I believe is very beneficial, as the family feels they can contribute, and not that you are in the room alone, mumbling some strange incantations of which they are not a part. I really like to have the family as involved as possible, as we are there not to take over but as a help to the dying person and, the more the family can partake in the death of their loved one, the more it also helps the grieving process later. This is all up to the dying person, naturally.

It is important to be aware of, and have respect for, all members of the grieving family and to make sure they also understand that what you do has already been agreed by their dying loved one. To this end, I always ask the dying person if it is all right for the family to be there while I am explaining to them what my service is.

You can suggest that a member of the family may help with the washing of the body and dressing it later for the coffin. They may also like to celebrate in some of the prayers. Inclusion of the family is important. Be extra sensitive to their vulnerability at this sad time for them and do not impose any of your beliefs.

It is also a very good idea, if there are grandchildren or young adult relations of whom the dying person approves, that they make the coffin, if the body is going to be buried. This can be done with joy and a sense of great appreciation for the dying relative, depicted by the way in which the coffin is decorated, e.g., if the person loved cats or dolphins, the coffin can be painted with them.

I know of a situation where the dying mother asked to see her coffin made and beautifully painted in the brightest colours by her two teenage children. The children told me later that it was the most important thing they could have done for their mother.

Care of the Environment
When a Person Is Dying

It is important to realize that the consciousness of the dying person is expanding into the whole of the room as they release the material world more and more. It is important to know that our consciousness transcends death. This means that the dying are much more sensitive to external impressions and their senses are magnified. I suggest that the following may be helpful:

- Remove all scented flowers, candles and incense, replacing them with unscented flowers, a white candle (symbolizing a return to innocence) and sandalwood incense (because of its purifying essence).

- Electric lights should be switched off. However, a small violet or orange light may be lit, as these help the life force to travel out of the body towards the head exit.

- Crying and loud sounds are not permitted in the room, as silence is essential.

- I believe that music is also a distracting element. If an initiated *Anam-Áire* is present, s/he will be sounding the soul's note and that is sufficient.

- As the senses of the dying person are heightened as death approaches, it is therefore essential that any thoughts one might have regarding the dying person are those of kindness and love.

- The sense of hearing is the last to disappear; speaking in the room is not advisable, as words can be irritating to the ethereal nervous system.

- When the person is going through the last stages of dying, i.e., when the breath is erratic and they are drifting more and more from this world, it is inadvisable to touch the body. For many dying people, the skin becomes ultra-sensitive, so touching is again intruding on their auric field.

- Please remember that, even though the elements may not have been able to contain consciousness any longer, the secondary or shadow body still vibrates, so be very careful about all the above suggestions.

Throughout the watching time with the dying person, you will have been aware of how the body is lying in the bed and usually it is in a straight posture in the end. If the relatives are not opting for funeral undertakers to cleanse and dress the body, you need not be concerned about doing these rituals for at least three hours after the soul has left. The head may have dropped to the side a little and that is fine. Let it be for now. If you find for any reason that the body is very twisted, it is in order to ask permission to reverently move the body a little, and do so with minimum intervention. People worry in case rigor mortis sets in quickly. I have no such worry and am happy to talk with relatives about this.

As a watcher, you will remain in the room after the body has departed and you will have negotiated the procedures with the family before the death takes place, so that everyone knows what to expect. If the dead person had been at home for the past few months, most of the immediate grieving will have been done. By this I mean they will have had time to say goodbye and have settled their business together. When the death happens, the family are neither in shock nor in the trauma of the death, as they will have done most of their crying and other expressions of grief will have been allowed expression. This is not to say, however, that they will not grieve at the final passing of their loved one, but they will not have to do what Elisabeth Kübler-Ross calls "grief work". Naturally, they will want to stay in the room for as long as they wish and can assist you in your service.

How Can We Best Support the Dying?

"I can't give you back your strength
I can't bring you back your breath
I can't bring you back your years to live again
I can't take away this pain.

I can't go this road with you
This is something only you must do
I can't break the ice of all the frozen years
But I can hold you in your fears.

I can't make your dreams come true
Can't bring your life back for you
But I can give to you
the only thing that's mine
I'll share with you my time.

I sit and watch with you
My tears are flowing too
The beauty of your soul
in tune with mine.
I hear a gentle sigh
I sing my lullaby
You're flying high
This is goodbye
Goodbye."

The words of this song may be useful when watching with the dying. I composed it at the bedside of a dear friend in Derry, Northern Ireland.

People nowadays are usually well supported medically and mentally in both hospitals and hospices. The latter deals very well with both aspects of care to also include pastoral or spiritual care.

Hospitals I have found do a wonderful job medically in compassionate physical care and loving mental care; that is their main emphasis of course. But is that enough?

To offer spiritual care, and by that I mean support for their soul, would necessitate more trained staff and as in most hospital care units, this is not a financial option. But I have seen nurses shape-changing into angels in some hospitals and hospices. These women and men answer an inner passionate devotion to their vocation. Usually a priest or minister will offer prayers (and extreme unction if the dying person is Catholic which can be very comforting to the dying, as I saw when my mother was dying)) to dying patients and this is very helpful to many. I was very surprised though that my dying father did not ask for a visitation from a priest even though he was a Catholic. I had noticed this also with other practising Christians. One story to illustrate this is the following:

Rose, a woman of 67, was dying from kidney failure and was quite weak. I was "doing the rounds" in the unit and the nurse let me know that Rose wanted me to sit by her and I was happy to do so. The following took place:

Me . . . My name is Phyllida and I'm happy to sit here by your bed, Rose. I usually visit ill people and often pray with them or just listen to any worries or concerns they might have.

Rose . . . (not her name) Oh good, Millisa! (my name is not so usual thus the problem in naming me!) I need something done but I don't want my family to know. After I die they will know.

Me . . . How can I help then, Rose?

She seemed stressed so I said:

Me . . . Would it make it easier to hold my hand when you tell me? And remember, I may not be able to do as you suggest.

Rose . . . Ok. After I die I would like you to tell the family what I've asked you to write.

Me . . . No problem, let me know what it is, Rose, please.

Rose . . . John is not my son. I reared him as mine but his own mother Mary, my cousin, is in another part of the country. I'll explain it in the letter, in the hope you'll write and give it to Jane, my sister.

Me . . . I'm happy to do that Rose. I'll pull the curtain so we can be very private.

I did so and wrote the sad story. Then as I read it back to Rose, tears filled her eyes.

Me . . . How do you feel, Rose?

Rose . . . I wish I had told this story before in person to the family and to John in particular.

Me . . . I'd be happy to call your family, including John, and ask them to please come next week and you can let them know the story. How does that feel, Rose?

Rose . . . Do you not think it is too late now?

Me . . . Not if you want this to happen.

Rose . . . Would you be here with me when I tell them? I couldn't do it alone.

Me . . . Yes, I'll be here with you and the family members who can come. (Rose had a sister and a brother; her husband had died in a car accident two years before; she had four children including John.)

So the story had a most healing ending. We sat by Rose's bed. I pulled over the curtains and I introduced myself, let the family know why we were together and Rose slowly told the story. At the end of which John came forward. Rose held him, they embraced as the family cried together. I believe they were tears of relief. John said he always felt a "pull" towards "Mary" (his biological mother) but also felt the love from Rose and the rest of the family.

Rose died 10 days after this blessed event and John thanked me for having been with Rose and them all. "I feel real peace now, Phyllida" he shared with me. "No more skeletons in the cupboard."

This was John's farewell letter to Rose which was left in the coffin …

"Thank you, mother, for giving me all the life I have lived so far. Now it's up to me to live the rest of it as well."

I kept in touch with the family and the last I heard was that John met with Mary again. This time to hear the whole story from her angle. Seemingly they meet often since Rose died and all is well.

The lesson for me in this was . . . here and now is the place to share what might lie heavy in our hearts on our death beds.

"Don't wait, I hear you say

Until your dying day,

before you do the things

you need to do.

If there are things undone

Before your life is gone

Do them now

Say them now

Live them now."

Guidelines for Helping the Dying

You can help the dying in so many ways. Be sure you respect them well.

1. You always ask their permission before you intercede in any way. Total respect for their needs is important.

2. Do not promise what you can't deliver . . . no big offers you cannot follow through.

3. Always ask the dying gently, slowly, clearly if they need anything from you rather than suggesting you give them something, e.g., massage their head, hands etc.

4. Always lower your voice when you are with them. Speak clearly, and never stand in front of them when you engage with them. This is too overpowering. Stand to the left side when connecting and never lean over them, again overpowering.

5. Do not just take it for granted they need to hold your hand, especially towards the end when they cannot converse with you. Touch is too intrusive at this stage. Consciousness is expanding so everything to do with the senses is magnified.

6. Flowers and candles are distracting for the one who is trying to complete their inner journey without form. Too many artefacts around the room are not helpful, especially incense and smelling roses or lilies.

7. Swabs of cool but not cold water dipped in diluted glycerine may help cracked lips. And cool, not cold compresses help when the body is heating up when the fire energy is de-cathexing. (A term used when the energy is dissipating.)

8. Always know beforehand what spiritual path, if any definite one, the dying person follows before praying at the bedside and if none then ask if there are any words like a poem or a script that would help them that they would like to have repeated to them as they are dying.

I remember an incident that occurred when I was living in Northern Ireland (I lived there for 26 years during the "troubles"):

I had been visiting an elderly woman in a hospital in Derry city and she was dying with heart failure. I asked her if she had a spiritual practice that I could support her in. Her answer was, "Yes please, Phyllida." Here is the way the conversation went.

Me . . . I'm happy to help in any way I can, Joan (her name was not Joan).

Joan . . . My friend goes to your yoga class and you said you don't have to go to church to live a good life. I don't. You said too that everyone is spiritual anyway.

Me . . . Yes, I believe this, Joan.

Joan . . . I'm Protestant. You know we don't say the rosary.

Me . . . That's fine, Joan. You don't have to. Is there any way you'd like me to help you today?

Joan . . . There is. You know the rosary, don't you? Would you say the rosary with me?

Me . . . Of course, I will, Joan.

And I did! And she reminded me to say "amen" after the salutations to Mary!

The night nurse shared with me later that Joan asked one of the doctors who was Catholic (everybody knew the other person's religious practice) if he had a set of rosary beads, and he gave her his. They were in her hands when her staunch Protestant family came to visit her the next day.

They took the beads away and Joan was in a very traumatic state when I saw her three days later. I called the family and shared with them that Joan wanted the beads as they brought her some kind of comfort fingering them, just like when they were small children they had a comfort blanket or a dummy or something small that they liked to have in their hands...It didn't make sense to drag a dirty blanket all over the house and the dummy that didn't have milk in it, but when we are small children these were important things. And often when we are dying we may revert at times of fear, to childhood ideas. Amazingly enough Joan's sister said . . .and I quote, "Ah well, we can live with that ok but if we thought our Joan was turning (phrase used when a Protestant "turned" Catholic, and vice versa) and her dying, we would never be able to face the neighbours again and our parents would (and again the phrase in another context) turn in their grave."

Joan died one month later. They asked me to place the rosary beads in her hands, which she fingered daily, but please, under the sheet. I did that.

9. Do not try too hard to fulfil all the needs of dying people. It is impossible to do this. Do what you can to see that they are physically comfortable and not too drugged with too much medicine. If they ask for music, ask what kind. If you can get it, fine, if not then maybe another piece by the same musician will do.

10. It is not necessary that dying people be washed all over twice a day. They need to be left in peace without disturbing their very tired bodies and minds. Nor is it helpful to offer antibiotics to the dying . . .the result of which intake leaves them in discomfort. I've seen thin flesh-less small arms of dear dying people being injected with antibiotics because they had kidney dysfunction. My suggestion is to make sure the patient is physically comfortable, conscious and not too much disturbed by ingestion of medicines to keep them so-called "alive" or food they may not want. I have written before that the digestion of food during the dying process is not only not necessary, but uncomfortable physically and keeps the soul grounded in a body it is hoping to depart from and move into the expansiveness of consciousness.

Most hospices and hospitals I have visited in the past few years operate from a consciousness of deep compassion and wisdom. They seem to adapt the philosophy that no one should die in severe pain, that painful deaths need not occur. And anyway, a lot of the pain of dying is not physical and I write about just that in my book, *The Last Ecstasy of Life*.

Let the dying person know they are loved before they become unconscious. When my father was dying, one night I sat by his bed when my siblings had gone to bed and I spoke with him. I said my hand was nearby if he wanted to hold it (he was not at all a demonstrative man and certainly not one for holding hands, so I left the decision to him). I was surprised when he reached for my hand. I gently held it. This was the conversation we had:

Me . . . Dad I'm sorry that just as I'm getting to know you, you are dying. I wish I had known you better. It was not easy for you with your inner struggles with your addiction. I often heard your cries in the night. I could feel your deep hurts. It must have been difficult being so in need of alcohol. I used to hurt for you and wished as a wee one that I could have helped. But I was afraid of you as a small vulnerable child. I want you to squeeze my hand if you are ok with me talking like this . . .

My Father gently pressed my hand.

Me . . . Thank you, dad. I wish you could forgive yourself for the sad, bad, bad times. I release you of all blame and I'm working on being free. You don't have time now to heal it all, but I do offer you my forgiveness. I'm going to be fully healed and I pray you will be too. You can choose to heal.

My father squeezed my hand and sighed. I saw a lone tear at the side of his eye.

Me . . . My heart opened with so much love for him. I felt the freedom that releasing someone from their guilt can bring.

As I write these words, I feel that tear at the side of my own eyes. Go well Father, into self-forgiveness at last. Go into the innocence that we all are. And then when you decide to heal with me, we will sing out together, you in your fine beautiful tenor voice, me in my older folk voice . . . *bheir mé ohh* . . . Carry me over.

Often people change their religious affiliations in life and many go on different spiritual journeys to the one taught them in childhood. Here is one story relating to this. I was introduced to Jo who was 75 years old and critically ill, suffering from kidney failure in a hospice. When I visited him, at his request, he mentioned that he no longer believed in the God of his religion which was Methodist. This was the sharing between us:

Jo . . . The problem is, Phyllida, most of my family are unaware of this except my younger sister who knows my "secret" and I don't want to hurt the others by letting them know. I'll let them go ahead with the funeral plans and have the church service they all talk about and want. I'll not be there anyway, so it doesn't matter, it's for them. I heard that you do rituals at funerals and marriages etc. Is there a private ritual you could do for me that doesn't have prayers…churchy prayers in it… something more down to earth, literally, would be wonderful. One of the doctors here talked about you doing a wedding ritual for his sister and it was not religious.

Me . . . Of course Jo, I'd be delighted and honoured to do a ritual for you. You can let me know how you would like it to be. Your own input is all important. If there are any artefacts like maybe a stone, branch, letter, photo, garment, card, piece of jewellery, CD or anything at all that you would like to put on your altar then we can obtain these things from your sister with whom you could share your idea of a ritual.

So, Jo's sister was very happy to bring some small artefacts that were precious to Jo, because she understood him better than the rest of the family. And we arranged a date for the sacred ritual to which his sister would act as witness.

I placed the artefacts on a small table near the bed and as Jo loved the earth and all in it, I brought the following:

- One container with water, representing the fluids in his physical body;
- One with earth representing his physical form;
- One with a candle which would be lit later representing the fire of passion;
- One with a feather representing air, his breath; and
- Incense representing space and consciousness that pervades all reality.

I asked Jo if he had anything to say to these great elements in his nature and in all nature. His considered reply which he had thought about the morning before was:

"I dedicate my body and all the elements in it to the earth that gave it to me."

I invited Jo to light the candle and offer it as gratitude to the breath that sustained him all his life. He did so and asked that the great mother earth would go with his spirit to the world of mystery. We all said *"Seá"*. Jo was very happy to give the candle to his sister to light it in the church.

It is so important to be able to in some way have the wishes of dying people come true and it does not take a lot sometimes to do so. One need only use one's creative power, soul, to bring rituals to those who request them.

Technology Can Help People Suffering Alone in Hospital

I was very honoured a few months ago when I was asked if I might help in a hospital with people seriously ill, but not on a ventilator, with Covid. I was happy to compose a song which I am glad to say helped in a small way to comfort these people. I am also happy to hear that it comforted the relatives as well, to the extent that they sang it when they went home from the hospital, and some sang it over and over together. The words of this song are:

> "You're not alone
> I'm watching here
> Breathe in the love
> Breathe out the fear
> My hand is near
> beside your own
> I tell you now
> You're not alone.
>
> And you're not alone
> Though night has come
> Your angel friend
> carries you home
> You're safe to leave
> You're safe to stay
> Follow your soul
> She knows the way.
> You're not alone."

It is also important that people in hospital during this time of pandemic are able to hear the voices of the relatives. And so messages spoken by means of FaceTime or WhatsApp can be really important, can bring them near. Photographs are also very important in these situations as oftentimes the faces of our dear ones are not so clear when we have to consume much medication. Even if they cannot name their relatives in the photographs, images of their faces can bring great comfort.

Photographs together with familiar sounds, such as children's voices, the dog at home barking, relatives talking together, sounds of waterfalls, crunching leaves under our feet, sounds of bird-song, all help to keep the person present and connected to the family and friends. One woman told me, that it was the sound of her dog barking on a recorder sent to her that comforted her the most. That, followed by a photograph of her dog Daisy, gave her great hope. Recordings of songs that the patient knew, also help them in their lonesome time.

We did an exercise in our community of making blessing branches, which is an Irish way of blessing through weaving colours on to a branch, each colour representing a blessing. The relatives held these branches and put their own blessings into them. The patients could then hold the branches and feel connected to their family. We also suggested that relatives and their children make soft fabric representations of the heart sending love from their hearts to the relatives in hospital, this was also a great comfort.

When it is not possible for relatives to visit their dead relatives in the hospital, creating a simple ritual for the loved person at home can be comforting. Many people mourn a lot at these rituals where the body of the deceased is not present. And that is so healing for them all. When I took such a ritual in the past, I found that the fact that the body was not present was a source of a deeper agony for the dear bereaved people.

RICUAL
CO SAY GOODBYE

Place an article or artefacts belonging to the deceased or associated with them, on a table, in a spare room or, if that is not available, in a special place in the living room, together with a lit candle, an up-to-date photograph, and flowers that they might have loved or a pot plant that they liked.

The family takes turns to stand at the table (standing makes it more formal and therefore more ceremonial. And that is actually important for people if they do not or cannot go to church). They share with the others what they loved most about the deceased, any funny episodes they remember, or a story that they experienced with the beloved, before they had to go to hospital.

The table may remain as an altar for three days during which time the bereaved may visit it and either pray or just sit in silence and be with the beloved in silence.

If the people are religious, they may want to finish with a well-known prayer or if they do not have a spiritual practice, they can offer a wish or a blessing for the departed.

It is also important that the family can embrace one another and have a meal together to keep the connection.

Sacred Ritual
of Watching with the Dead

Your own practice of daily meditation and visualization is all-important in this service of Watching with the dying.

- Sit comfortably in your chair, close your eyes, and withdraw from the outside world.

- Be in touch with your breathing without changing it. Allow your body to relax totally into your breath.

- In a relaxed inner place of peace, breathe in peace, let it travel throughout your body, send the peace to the dead person and visualize them receiving it.

- It is not your peace that you give them, but you share in the peace already available always and which is ready to be received.

The following **prayer** may be said at this stage:

"Dear soul of love,

know that you are no longer in bodily form.

Allow yourself to be totally at peace.

Allow this peace to fill your mind completely,

So that the dear earth-mind may be transformed into love.

Allow this peace to travel with you on and on,

Until you reach your place of union with the Beloved."

- Visualize the soul travelling on further from earth existence, on and on towards the love and light of its own beauty and holiness. Keep your mind on this steadily, without any form of distraction whatsoever. The more you can stay with the visualization, the more beneficial the watching will be for the soul. When you have stayed here in this place of uninterrupted visualization, which should take about one hour, notice if there are any interruptions, notice any disturbance. If you do, keep on repeating the above prayer until you feel the peace stream in again.

- Now, slowly move from the chair. Walk in an anti-clockwise circle (if there is room behind the bed) **smudging or smoking the sandalwood incense** around the bed, three times repeating the words:

"I ask that all attachments

And all connections to the material worlds

Be broken now

In the name of Brigid, Jesus and your Guardians.

(Or to whomsoever they had had devotion)

Amen. Alleluia. *Seá*."

- Sit down again and now regain your presence of mind as you **visualize the soul meeting with its guides and wise counsellors.**

- See the soul shining and joy-filled.

- Feel what is happening.

- Is the dead person peaceful and going on with this stage or do you get a sense that they are still perhaps looking back to the earth plane?

- Obey your own intuition in this and, if you feel you ought to do the releasing of earth energy again, then do so as often as you deem necessary. This stage could take an hour to complete.

- Sit down slowly again in your chair and breathe into your solar plexus and, with a deep out-breath, breathe out any resistance you may have felt at the last stage.

- Relax totally and then visualize the soul being shown a video, so to speak, of the person's whole life.

Notice any attitudes of self-disgust or inappropriate guilt, which is self-judgment. These mean that the earth-mind is still present and is preventing further progress. (Whilst it is natural for us to have regrets for having done some unkindly deeds, it is inappropriate that we should criticize ourselves.)

With the following **prayer**, you pray that the soul may embrace the ego towards forgiveness and mercy:

"Dear one, with deep love

And deep compassion for your ego-mind,

Help it now to let go of any attitudes of self-loathing,

Help it to see your life from a place of motherly love,

Help it to see its own innocence shining,

So that any self-judging

May be transformed into love.

Amen, Alleluia, *Seá*."

- Now take in a deep breath and **chant "Ah"** as you breathe out towards the bed.

- Take a drink of water and visualize the following: Imagine the soul helping the earth-or conditioned-mind to release its trespasses and so create peace within itself and all around. Get a sense of the guides and helpers rejoicing as the soul reviews the past life and sees the ways whereby it can redress the "mist-aches" and with love and self-tolerance move on. This stage may take another hour.

If the family are present, they may take part in the next stage (You will have already arranged with them what is to be done, naturally.):

- Have someone **light a white candle** and have him or her place it beside the other one already lit. They then say these words of **prayer**:

"May the light of your own bright soul

Go on towards the great white light

Of unconditional love, that awaits you, dear one.

Know that we have no ties to you.

Know that we send you gracefully and with joy

To the marriage-feast of you and beloved spirit.

All is forgiven; your own love awaits you.

Amen, Alleluia, *Seá*."

- Having made this prayer, s/he now sits down on a chair (already placed there by the watcher) to the left side of the door.

- Another family member may now take the **incense or sage from the altar** and with three clockwise, circular movements of their right hand towards the corpse, they say the following **prayer**:

> "May the sweet fragrance of purifying grace abide in you.
>
> May the guardians of honour and peace attend you.
>
> May you be blessed in the mercy of your own divinity.
>
> May the blessing of Brigit (and whomsoever) now go with you.
>
> May all beings be raised because of your life in earth this time."

- They now leave the incense on the altar and sit to the right of the door.

- The watcher again goes deep within her/himself and visualizes the scene clearly. Having sensed the scene, she now visualizes the soul leaving the place of review and being slowly led by its guides and guardians of souls to a place of rest for a while. They are safely carried in, all is well. They will rest here in this place of loving awareness for some time (again, we use the term "time", although we know that in the place of spirit time, is not relevant). This may last for one hour of our time.

- Then the watcher recites the **incantation** for the dead person (see p. 126).

The first three hours will now have expired, so it is time for the watcher to go outside the room, but she must do so in a very respectful and ritualistic way. Firstly s/he bows towards the corpse, and then to the right, to the left, and behind her/him, thus acknowledging the four directions and four elements. Then s/he slowly walks backwards towards the door, bows again and leaves. Once outside s/he does not talk to anyone, as s/he is still in an altered state of consciousness. Having drunk water and eaten some food, s/he then goes outside in nature for one hour. All the while, s/he is alone, with no talking and no quick movements. The other prestigious people or relatives may want to be in the room, either praying or holding vigil of meditative silence.

This is as far as the watcher can take the soul on its journey. An initiated *Anam-Áire* continues the journey for another two days, not always in the same room as the corpse, as the watching may be done from another place altogether (even from another country).

Incantation for the Dead Person

This incantation for the dead person may be recited by family members as long as they do not get emotionally involved. Detached love and compassion are the emotions necessary for this work.

In the past, the incantation has been chanted only by the *Anam-Áire* and has been done so every hour for the first three hours after death, and then every three hours thereafter for three days. It is to be said slowly or chanted with the full attention on every word.

I am happy that sensitive lay-people should have access to these rituals of passage and I am honoured to pass them down in both written form and orally, as in the case of an initiated *Anam-Áire*.

Be sure you will not be distracted by anyone. Light your candle and wear your holy stole if you are a priest/ess.

The Incantation

"Dear soul, I sit with you as you journey towards the centre of love.

I urge you to travel on past the dark avenues of your own common mind's making.

Travel on past envy and greed, past sexual needs and poverty, past longing of the flesh for food and water.

Go on past the common mind's rages and lusts, past regrets and remorse.

Travel on past all unfinished courses, past stormy words of passion and ice-cold heart of lost dreams.

Go on past the red and orange of sunset, past yellow of sunrise, past the green pastures of desiring,

Past the ragged skies of your disharmony,

Past the purple discontent of your thoughts.

Go on and on; do not stop, do not look back to earth. It is no longer your home.

Be not disturbed by song or dance, by what appears to be love and joy; they do not exist: they are unreal.

Go on past yesterday and today, past tomorrow and all futures that may present themselves to you.

Go on past all births, past maybes and possibilities.

Go on past male and female, past youth and decay, past the skeletons
of bloody battle and warring faces.

Travel on past all breaths and sounds, all touch and taste,

Past all human values that distract your voyage.

Go on past all belonging of your clay body, all clay connections,

Past grief and anger, past jealousies and hatreds,

Past all clinging and attachments.

Go on past all knowledge and philosophies; carry on past human
tendencies and human aversions,

Past the call of your family alive and dead,

Past the call of your ancestors.

Go on past all illnesses and suffering, past all possessions and
strivings, past successes and failures.

Travel on and on past your own sad or happy projections,

Past tears and sorrowing.

Travel on and on inward into the place where no thing and no person,
no feelings and no memory, can reach.

On and on to the place where only transparent light
of the one true spirit resides.

Go on through the seductive coloured veils of separation, on through
the magnetic voices of angels.

Go on through the 4th vibration, see through the hall of symphonies
the bright rainbow of colourful lights.

Go on past seductive smiles and on until at last you come to
the clear white shore

Where nothing calls you anymore and where no memory
can recall you,

Where nothing is outside or around you,

Where nothing disturbs your peace and calm.

Hear the voice of your own beauty, your own mirror, your own clear
love, call you softly home,

Home to be and rest for a while and no going out.

No more standing at the threshold waiting for exit.

Now you can be at one with your own soul love,
no more wandering out.

No more to take the sorrowing flesh to cover your soul.

No more to breathe the air of distraction and forgetting.

Only love, pure and gold, breathes you now.

I can take you no further now. Go on into love.

Go on until you have reached the clear shore of love's embrace.

I leave you now in the arms of love.

All grace be with you.

May all beings be blessed because of this greeting
and incantation. *Seá*."

Blessing the Body

There will be no problem regarding identification of celebrants for the ritual, as this will have been discussed with the dying person whilst they were still consciously aware. The two people chosen to help will have prepared the room beforehand. The two watchers stand at the bottom of the bed and say an appropriate prayer such as:

"We give thanks

For the honour of preparing this body

For its return to Earth.

May all grace attend us

And may all life be blessed

Because of this ritual.

Amen, Alleluia, *Seá*."

A basin of water, not hot, to which a little sage and lavender will have been added, will be near the bed, with two cloths soaking in it. The two towels will be beside it. A change of clothes will also be over a chair next to the bed.

The two watchers will now take up their place of service at either side of the bed. They take down the covers and, gently and reverently, together remove the clothes from the corpse. These may be left in a basket. Starting at the feet, appropriate prayers may be said as each part of the body is washed. One watcher may start the prayer and the second one adds the blessing:

Feet

Prayer: We give thanks for the feet that walked many miles and experienced many journeys. For the journeys not taken we release you. All is forgiven.
Blessing: We now bless them and give thanks.

Belly

Prayer: We give thanks for the belly that held power and strength to continue incarnating. For the times of overpowering others, all is forgiven.
Blessing: We now bless it and give thanks.

Abdomen

Prayer: We give thanks for the abdomen that let go of fear and jealousy. For the times of envy and arrogance, all is forgiven.
Blessing: We now bless it and give thanks.

Legs

Prayer: We give thanks for the legs that followed the path of righteousness and kindness. For the times they followed only self-interest, all is forgiven.
Blessing: We now bless them and give thanks.

Thighs

Prayer: We give thanks for the thighs that led the body in the direction of the soul.
For the times they led only to stress and sorrow, all is forgiven.
Blessing: We now bless them and give thanks.

Genitals

Prayer: We give thanks for the genitals that gave gender to the body, so it might love fully. For the times of lustful pursuits only, all is forgiven.
Blessing: We now bless them and give thanks.

Breasts

Prayer: (If the corpse was female:)
We give thanks for the breasts that fed life. For the times of dishonouring them, all is forgiven.
(If the dead person is male, one might pray:)
We give thanks for the giving of your protection and support. For the times of selfish pursuit only, all is forgiven.
Blessing: We now bless them and give thanks.

Heart

Prayer: We give thanks for the heart that beat in this body. For the times it felt resentment and revenge, all is forgiven.
Blessing: We now bless it and give thanks.

Throat

Prayer: We give thanks for the throat that spoke words of loving kindness. For the words of love not spoken, all is forgiven.
Blessing: We bless it and give thanks.

———

Ears

Prayer: We give thanks for the ears that heard the word of wisdom and followed it. For the times when they listened to other voices and not their own, all is forgiven.
Blessing: We bless them and give thanks.

———

Hands

Prayer: We give thanks for the hands that gave from their bounty and received from their joy. For the times of greed and withholding, all is forgiven.
Blessing: We bless them and give thanks.

———

Arms

Prayer: We give thanks for the arms that enfolded another in friendship and pain. For the times of rejecting and abandoning, all is forgiven.
Blessing: We bless them and give thanks.

———

Shoulders

Prayer: We give thanks for the shoulders that carried the burdens of life with courage. For carrying too many burdens, thus causing one stress, or relinquishing burdens, all is forgiven.
Blessing: We bless them and give thanks.

———

Neck

Prayer: We give thanks to the neck that turned the head in the direction of the light. For the times when it turned away from the light, all is forgiven.
Blessing: We bless it and give thanks.

———

Eyes

Prayer: We give thanks for the eyes that gazed with compassion on all life. For the times when they looked with disdain and hatred, all is forgiven.
Blessing: We bless them and give thanks.

———

Nose	**Prayer:** We give thanks for the nose that smelt life in all its fragrance. For the times when it could not sense anything, all is forgiven. **Blessing:** We bless it and give thanks.

———————

Mouth	**Prayer:** We give thanks for the mouth that fed this body and spoke words of comfort to others. For the times it refused to take in life or spoke with unlove, all is forgiven. **Blessing:** We bless it and give thanks.

———————

Top of the Head	**Prayer:** We give thanks for the head and all it perceived in life. For what it could not understand, all is forgiven. **Blessing:** We bless it and give thanks.

———————

Now that the body has been washed (this washing is symbolic rather than practical), dried and blessed, the watchers begin to dress it anew. Remember that the body will be quite heavy in death, as there is no cooperation from the corpse. The feet may be drawn close together, the hair can be combed and the hands placed together on the chest. Up until a few years ago the body was plugged to prevent leakage of any dislodged faeces or, if there had been internal bleeding, sometimes blood escaped from the orifices of the body. This is not a practice carried out these days, as most people do not eat for many days before death. Sometimes a sanitary pad is applied to the body in case of leakage.

The corpse or body is now lying straight in the bed, as this facilitates the lying in the coffin. As was made clear to the relatives and family, the watcher's work is now complete; they may, however, remain in the room and pray until other members of the community come to pay respects.

The *Anam-Áire* continues to pray her/his prayers and intercessions for another three days thus following through to the last *Áite*.

Disposing of Water and Bedclothes

Disposing of the Water the Body Was Washed With

When the body has been washed, the water is kept in the basin until such time as it can be disposed of. Bring the water to the root of a tree and as you pour it into the earth say the following words:

"May the water that cleaned the earth body of (name the person) be
a source of nourishment for the earth which now receives it. In the
name of the mother and father who bore you. In the name of the soul
that lived, breathed, and had its being in you, I pour this water now
into the earth.
Amen, Alleluia, *Seá*."

Burning of the Bedclothes after a Death

Having taken off the clothes from the body and having placed them in a basket, as suggested, leave them in a drawer until after the funeral. Some people like to make this the final "letting-go ritual" and friends are called to support them. They may ask the support of a dear friend of the deceased to carry the basket to the fire or ask them to bring matches, etc. Some people ask a friend to officiate at the ritual, so that they only take part in what is relevant to them. This is also a deep blessing for all.

Together with the bedclothes, bring some sage or sandalwood to the fire already burning. Burn the clothes whilst praying the following prayer:

"May these clothes, which covered our dear one, (naming them),
burn in the fires of transformation. May her/his soul be free from all
earth matter and may her/his memory be a blessing to all
whom s/he encountered in the earth.
Amen, Alleluia, *Seá*."

As the clothes are burning, throw some sage or sandalwood into the flames and pray the following:

> "I give thanks for the life of my dear (friend, husband, father, etc.).
> I pray that, as the last piece of clothing is being burnt in the fires of
> transforming love, we be blessed by the cleansing fires of grace in
> our souls. You no longer need clothing of earth to cover your spirit.
> May you be free in your spirit life.
> Amen, Alleluia, *Seá*."

When all has been burnt, reflect for a while in reverence for the life now ex-carnated and then leave the site, having cleared the earth around the fire, ready for the next burning ritual.

Burial of Rings

The spouse of the deceased celebrates this ritual whenever they decide the time is right to do so. This may be immediately after the burial of their spouse or it may take place years after. It is witnessed and supported by whomsoever they desire to have present. Often, the people who were present at the wedding are witnesses.

The woman/man taking the ring to a place already prepared goes on her/his knees on the earth.

Whilst in a kneeling position, s/he digs a small hole with her/his fingers. S/he then places the ring in the hole whilst saying the following prayer:

"With love and honouring of our wedding day,
in memory of the life we spent together and the love we shared,
I now place this ring in the earth with joy and happy memories of
when you placed it on my finger until death did us part."

Whilst covering the ring with earth they continue:

"May the earth use the gold in this ring to provide nurturing
for the clay and may I be blessed by her in this ritual of
letting-go and transformation.

May I be released from any vows and promises made to you
in this lifetime and may I be free to live my life from now on in
detached love until we meet again."

Now stay a short while in reverent reflection and then leave the place.

Letting Go of the Past

Whilst this ritual is mainly for those having done their grief-work after the death of a loved one, it may also be used by anyone needing to release from any kind of relationship and get on with their lives. Feel free to use this exercise in the way that suits you best, using the appropriate wording.

letting-go Ritual

Place an article or photo/letter of the person whom you need to release on a small altar.

Place a white candle to the right of the article. Place a black candle to the left of it.

Put a dish of sage or sandalwood on the altar and burn it.

Place a dish with earth behind the article or photo.

You may have fresh flowers on the floor in front of the altar.

Sit comfortably on a chair and close your eyes. Give thanks that this ritual is available to you.

Visualize the person from whom you need to release standing in front of you but not too close. See them clearly without animosity; see them happy, and well (even if they have died).

Visualize yourself standing in front of them but not too close. See yourself without animosity, happy and well.

Call on your guides and wise ancestors to stand behind you, supporting you. These may include Jesus, if you wish.

Feel grounded and free.

Call on the guides and wise ancestors of the person you are releasing and ask them to stand behind them, supporting them.

Now light the black candle whilst saying aloud:

"I ask that this black candle, which symbolizes transformation and change, shine its light into the dark places in us."

Now light the white candle whilst saying aloud:

"I ask that this white candle, which symbolizes innocence and new beginnings, shine its light into the unclear parts of us."

And say out loud, slowly:

"I (naming yourself), do thank you, (naming the other), for the gift of your presence in my life. It is now timely that we separate and go our different ways. I release you in the name of love and gratitude. I release you in the name of Brigit, the releaser to new life. I release you in the name of all that is pure and good, That you be released into it and I be released into it, in the name of love."

Now placing the article or photo in the basin with the earth, say:

"I return this article of earth to the earth, that all connections with you, (mention the name again), may be severed in this life. What is left is a loving memory in my heart. Thank you for having taken a body in the earth. You are free to go from me now. I am free to go from you now. Amen, Alleluia, *Seá*."

Stay some time in prayer and thanksgiving, then blow out the candles and leave the room. Walk outside in silence for a few minutes in grateful reflection.

Return later and remove the candles from the altar, remove the dish of earth and place the article into the earth outside. The photograph or letter can be burned in the dish containing the sage and sandalwood and then the ashes returned to the earth.

I usually suggest that a small seedling be planted in the earth, so that a flower or tree may grow next year to celebrate the release with love.

Remove everything from the room, leaving it as you found it.

Distant Help for the Dying
through Imaging and Meditation

It is a well-known belief within our Celtic tradition that there is a thin veil between the worlds of creation and that we can be of great assistance to the souls passing over from body to spirit life. I had often heard my old Nanny McDyre talk about the "poor souls dying at this minute and no one there to help them pass over". Some years ago I got the feeling, as I was praying for a dying person, that I could also be of real assistance to a particular soul dying at that precise time. The idea came to me to go to them psychically, to look with my inner eye and see if they needed assistance in their dying process. This I did and felt a real sense of connection with the soul of this person who was dying and afraid to pass over. I also saw his relatives and friends and knew I could help them, too, from a place of detached yet compassionate love and care. Often, at times I felt that I knew the person who was either dying or who had died; the sense of connection was so immediate.

In a workshop in Stüttgart, I introduced this meditation. In it, I was shown the scene of a man dying in a car crash. I went to his aid and stayed with him, assuring him that he was in fact out of his body and was adjusting to another state of beingness. I was assured that his heart had stopped and that death was quick. I spoke aloud what I had seen internally and I suggested that one of the participants could go to the aid of the family and "help" them by sending them love and support as they heard of the news of their loved one's having died. This was done with ease and grace. Other participants were able to send immediate love and prayers.

Often during these meditations, the scenes before my eyes were so vivid that I could not believe they were not actually happening in material form. Then who is to say what is real and what is imagined? Our imaginations are but images that present themselves to us and the better we become at visualizing, the better able we are to enter into the other world of created phenomena.

This meditation is one that may be done at any time of the day or night; as mentioned before, if one awakens during the night, this is a good time to tune into this meditation. It is of deep service to another, which brings grace to the meditator and to the soul receiving it.

meditation

Sit comfortably on a chair with your body relaxed and quiet.

Become aware of the breath as it comes into your body-mind and leaves again.

Do this for the next five breaths, relaxing more and more as you do so. Follow the breath in and follow it out again.

Now allow your soul to open up to someone who is dying. Feel yourself expanding in consciousness and awareness of all around you as you sit with closed eyes.

Do not try to conjure up a situation where someone is dying but allow your imagination to take you to a place where it is happening.

As you begin to imagine or see images of the scene in front of you, follow carefully all that presents itself to you.

See the person who is dying. Where are they?

It may be a hospital scene, at home, an accident, or a sudden death. Do not change anything that presents itself to you; simply follow and be led by the scene.

Who is near them?

Are there relatives around? If so, what are they doing?

Now go to the person who is dying and be with them.

Open the heart of love in you to them and see their predicament. Are they in fear? Are they in pain?

Assure them gently that they are dying and that you are there to help them and tell them your name.

Sense what they are feeling and be empathic without sympathizing.

Be clear and give clear words to them, e.g., "You are at the side of a road and there has been an accident. You are bleeding from the head and you are dying" etc. Only relate what you sense, not what you think may be happening; you will learn to differentiate between these after some time.

Ask what they need now and let them know that they are safe, that they are leaving the body behind and all is well.

If they are still conscious, ask if they need some spiritual assistance, a prayer they like or know and would appreciate being said for them now.

Take time and pray. Do not be distracted.

If they become unconscious before medical help comes, and they die in your arms, speak words of comfort to them and assure them that the body is left behind, and that you are sitting by it, and it is no longer needed in order to go on with their life.

Be with their soul; keep assuring it that it is well, and encourage it to go on to the place waiting for it in spirit life.

When they have died, stay by the body, moving neither it nor yourself. Guide the soul to its guardians and keep repeating the words, "Go on, dear one; go on towards the light of your own grace and love. All is well."

If you can, wait here for some time and keep supporting the soul to release from earth life and be in the light of love's all-powerful holding.

If you are doing this meditation in a group, ask if someone might go to the family and/or children and comfort them whilst you watch with the soul on its journey. Speak aloud what is happening and one or two in the group will be able to go to the aid of the family. Stay in silence and reverence for fifteen minutes, and then slowly leave the scene when you sense that the guardians in the other life are caring for the soul.

When the meditation is over, stretch your body, yawn loudly, and open your eyes.

If you are in a group, you can all share the meditation, which normally takes one hour. Then finish with a song or your own prayer and give great thanks that you were called upon to be a watcher with the dying.

I advise that a special notebook be kept in which you enter all the watchings you do in a month. At the end of the month, read them through and meditate again for all the souls that have allowed you to be of assistance. You will be surprised just how many souls you will have helped.

Prayers for the Dead

Celtic Christians believed in praying for the dead, as I have already mentioned. They taught that the dead wait for our pleadings with God on their behalf to release them from suffering into the place of happiness. The Celts talked about the "Summerlands" and *Tir-na-nÓg* as a place of rest and great beauty, where the sun shone all the time. They believed that, when we die, we have the chance to come back again to live any parts of life not fully lived. Having come from the Indo-European countries, they brought with them the customs and religious beliefs and rituals pertaining to these lands. Reincarnation was therefore natural to the Celts, as their great love for the earth and all that lived in it predisposed them towards returning. It also answered their philosophy of respecting the innate order and rhythm in nature, that cyclical balancing of cause and effect that is reflected in all natural phenomena.

As the god of light also visited the underworlds, this meant the ego-minds there were never long without comfort. Of course, Jesus, who named himself the "light of the world", visited the underworld and brought comfort to all there, after he had "given up the ghost" or spirit. In a way, we are to believe that, in the darkest place in all the worlds of creation, a light shines. This is both comforting and reassuring for families who have had the sorrowing experience of suicide, or death by so-called accident, in the family.

And remember the words of Brigit:

"There is no one amongst you
Who is forgotten.
You only have to exchange
The heart of stone in you
For a heart of flesh.
Love will not force herself on you
But like a humble guest
Stands in your own shadow
Waiting for your invitation."

Prayers

For those who have no one to pray for them

"For those who have no one to pray for them,
We ask your guidance and love, oh Lord!
For those who have taken their lives into death,
We ask your guidance and love, oh Lord!
For those who are lost out there in the world
And cannot find their way home,
We ask your guidance and love, oh Lord!"

For those who took their own lives

"We ask your mercy on those who died in despair,
For the poor ones who had to finish their lives
By the doings of their own hands.
We ask your loving mercy for those that
Cannot find forgiveness for themselves.
Oh Lord! hear our prayer. Amen."

For those who have suffered in their passing

"Oh Love as wide as the oceans of the world!
Wrap yourself around our dear one (mention name),
And may the angels of good nature
Breathe softly on her/his brow
As they lullaby her/him to sleep
In the arms of comforting love." *Seá.*

143

For a sudden death

"May the arms of a loving mother gather them in.
May they know they are dead and be at peace.
May all the loving guides kneel around them
And call their name three times three
And may they answer and let go
And surrender to love's song."

Seá.

For the death of a child

"Ahh! Your passing splits us open (name the child);
Your small life with us
Brought a moment of joy
And we are learning
To breathe in moments now.
Your leaving us will bring us
Years dragging sadness behind us,
Time to mend the small sails
Of our windstorm boats.
Our joy amidst our pain
Is that you had no time
To grow in you
An earth-mind full of pride;
Your soul intact returns to love.
Help us to live our years with grace
So that wisdom
May whisper her reasons in our sleep."

Seá.

It is very important that you let your own prayers come through you. Why not sit down having read the prayers above and write your own prayers for your life into a journal titled "My prayers for my life". Add some, every day: prayers of gratitude, prayers of sadness, and prayers for others. We are too accustomed to having another provide us with prayers. This keeps us in the rôle of child in our relationship with the Divine. For me it is a bit like asking someone else to write a letter from you to a friend. Only you know what is in your heart, so begin to pray your own prayers and don't wait for a priest or minister to provide them. Remember that you are "the holy one of God/dess", so pray from that place of wholeness and speak with the authority of love in you. It is also important to give thanks for the lives of friends and relations who have died. When we offer thanksgiving for something, our own hearts swell in us and we are the recipients of joy and lightness. It is a Celtic practice to be grateful for all the blessings in our daily lives.

Of a grateful (great-full) heart, Brigit has this to say:

> "When the heart in you stretches in gratitude,
>
> The soul in you leaps for joy:
>
> When you spend your day in grumbling complaint,
>
> The soul in you bows her head."

I rather like the idea of my soul's leaping for joy as I give thanks for all the blessings in my day. That is not to say that we must only be giving thanks all the time. There is "a time for all things under heaven", as we know. A prayer I prayed some time ago in a deep pain was both healing and honest. I need to be honest in all my dealings, whether with the living or with spirit. I can get rather annoyed with my soul, too, when I perceive her taking too long to come to my aid! Only at a distance can I really see her workings in my life, and often I have to wait awhile before I can truly give thanks for her lessons. It is important that we do not pretend to ourselves that all is perfect, if that is not our belief at the time.

As I recall my Nanny McDyre, my heart swells in me and my energy rises with such gratitude for all she was and still is to me. Love never dies and the love with which we loved in bodily form still delights our souls. This love is divine; it cannot, and will never, die. A friend of mine, who was dying some years ago, looked up at me from her bed and smilingly said, "There's only love now, only love," and she closed her eyes and died in love. I believe that from a distance she saw her life and all that she experienced as a great blessing this time round.

145

Do What Is Natural

Naturally, if a person for whom you have a lot of love is dying, it is necessary to work through all the stages of your grieving. No two people grieve in the same way and it is always a gift to be given time to mourn before the person dies. Terminal illnesses give everyone the chance to grieve and let go before death, which is why it is so important to use this time to work through the feelings of loss and pain. It is not always easy to know how much grieving to do in the presence of the person who is experiencing the illness. Many relatives and good friends of the dying have said to me, "I can't go and see my dear friend who has been told the cancer is inoperable; it would break my heart. I would be no good to her/him. I want to remember them as they were. What will I do."

We all have our own ways of doing what is best at the time. It might be a good thing to ask your friend, etc., if s/he would like you to call. In most cases, the answer will be, "Yes, do please."

This is a very sad situation and one that many people go through. Somehow, I always feel that, whilst we try to be the best we can be for our friends (and that is great), we deny them and ourselves that deep intimacy of heart touching heart, soul deepening into soul, when we cannot allow them to see our vulnerability and brokenness, our love and our grief. Can you imagine the situation? Your dear friend or relative has been told they have but a short time to live; you hear the news and you are devastated, naturally. Your whole being wants to be with them; to hold them, to say you love them and that you are there for them; your tears are flowing all over your heart and face; you are in deep grief and possibly shock.

What is the natural thing to do? The Celts were a wonderful example of following the natural course of things instead of doing the so-called "right" thing. The right thing is usually the conditioned thing. Naturally, you want to be with your friend but your conditioned mind says, "No; wait until you pull yourself together, wait until you can be of some help to your friend, wait until you have done your grief work, wait until you have stopped this crying." In other words, wait until you are stronger and more in your head than in your heart. Fear of not being enough, of breaking down and making it worse for your friend, etc., keeps you back from doing what your heart asks you to do—to be with her/him in the way you always could be, no matter what life brought you both. Moreover, you wait and your friend/relative dies in their

146

sleep that night. Your grief will be more painful; your grief will now include self-judgment, self-blame and self-loathing and it will take longer to heal.

Can you imagine going to your friend/relative and both of you crying together with your arms around each other, sitting on the bed, sobbing your tears of loss, your tears of sorrow, together? This is the healing for you both; this is the time of great love and great pain, all wrapped up together in the warm embrace of vulnerability and authenticity. This is natural, and what is natural heals. Elisabeth Kübler-Ross, M.D., always maintained that "what is normal is not always natural". You can be with your loved one in that full and human way that does not pretend, gives no false hope nor takes hope away. It is being with what is and being able to be in each moment without trying either to fix it or change it. It is about life as well as death. It is the way of consciously living here and now in whatever is present in our lives.

Whilst it may seem totally unnecessary to make the following comment, I will, at the risk of sounding naïve, state that no matter how helpful or how healing your presence with the bereaved may be, you cannot and never will be able to give them what they want: their beloved back again in his/her health and well-being of body. It is important to bear in mind that all else you do, no matter how wonderful it may be, is always essentially secondary help, as you are helpless to deal with the bereaved person's primary need. Please remember that there is only so much you can do to be of real help. Your love and your willingness to be with what presents itself in the moment is more than sufficient. You must not tire yourself out in the process of caring for the dying or relatives as you will end up becoming ill yourself.

When leaving the bedside of the dying, I am often asked by the relative, "How do you think he looks today, Phyllida?" Somehow, I feel the pressure to answer in the positive. It is as if they are hoping you can produce some kind of miracle to make him better. My answer, if I feel it is appropriate is usually, "Well, he seemed without pain and less agitated," or, "I believe the medication is working well," or, "I imagine she will sleep now for a while," and I always follow this by asking if the relatives need any time with me to talk about things.

It is of great help to the bereaved if there is someone to do the practical things at the time of the death of a loved one. When one is going through emotional pain, it is difficult to concentrate on things like ordering wreaths, making food for the people coming from a distance to the funeral, registering the death, etc. A watcher's work is concerned with having regard for the spiritual welfare of the dying, and this is a concentrated and holy work; nevertheless, to be able to collect children from school, wash some dishes, collect a relative from the bus or train station, or care for the children, are all works of mercy and as such are holy. There is no hierarchy of holiness in this work. Someone asked me one time if she could help with the dying. I was delighted with her offer. When I asked if she could collect the dying woman's daughter from the train-station twenty miles away, the request was denied with the words, "I meant to be at the bedside of the dying, you know, to pray for them." We cannot all be at the bedside and a lot of the "work" I have done with the dying has been in the kitchen, making sandwiches for people visiting, or answering the phone and giving the information about time of cremation/burial, etc. I have a saying: "They also serve who stand and wash the dishes." Somehow it seems more "holy" to be at the bedside of the dying, rather than cleaning up the kitchen or doing the shopping for food, but everything we do at this time is "work" or help and nothing is too trivial in the line of service.

Many people ask me how long it "should" take before they get over the death of a loved one. My answer is always the same: "It takes as long as you take." I have heard some professionals say that the "normal" time for grieving is two years, after which time one "should" be able to get on with life. Naturally, it depends upon what the relationship with the deceased was and how the death happened; if it was a sudden death (as in heart attack), the shock will stay in the psyche for a longer time than if the person had had a terminal illness. Likewise, if death occurs through accident, the grieving time is more intense as the trauma of the suddenness has to be dealt with. It is crucial that we get to say goodbye to our loved ones before they die, as the guilt of "what I should have/have not said, what I should have/have not done" tortures the heart for so long. May we all have enough time to say our goodbyes and die consciously in the love of our dear ones, thus helping the grieving process for us and for them.

It is taught in the "Teachings from the Cauldron" that love never dies. This is the only reality which means that it alone is real for all times. This teaching helps me when working with people who did not get time to say goodbye to a loved one before they left the earth. Either of the exercises on the following page can be very healing.

My dear sister's young husband died after a car crash and she and their six young children were in shock for a long time. The fact that they were forbidden by relatives to open the coffin and make sure that it was the man they all loved who laid there, heightened their grief. "Supposing it is not Donal at all," my broken-hearted sister cried, "supposing he actually is still alive and the wrong man is lying there?"

All sorts of irrational thoughts crowd around, seeking some kind of hope or "maybe . . . ". Things have changed in our society since then; relatives get

a Farewell letter

Ask the bereaved person to write a letter of goodbye to the beloved deceased.

They can leave this letter on their little altar, with a night-light burning in front of it.

Or, they can place it under their pillow for three nights; then read it again and, if it feels right, they can burn it.

help to say goodbye

Ask the person to sit with a soft cushion in front of them.

This will represent the beloved, who died.

Let them know that the love they have for each other has not died.

Let them express all the feelings and all the words they did not have time to share. Tears and words of love and gratitude will be shared.

Allow this time of mourning as they take the cushion, hold it to their hearts, and cry out their sense of loss.

When all of this has been done and you feel it has been completed, ask them to say goodbye to their beloved. When they are ready to give you the cushion back, you then "derôle" it.

to see the corpse no matter how disfigured it might be, and I believe this is only right. For months after her husband died, my sister wanted to go to the graveyard, dig up the coffin and see for herself if it was actually his body.

Thankfully, she comes from a small community in Donegal, where we have the ritual of the "waking" of the corpse. This entails sitting up for three nights with the dead person, with their family and friends telling the story over and over again about how he/she died, the circumstances around the dying, every detail as to the last time they spoke to them, what was said, etc. This gave her the chance to tell the story of her husband's death repeatedly, until in the end she had to accept the fact that he had lived and had died.

The Celts believed that the story held great alchemy. Brigit said:

"Give voice to the story,

Give heart to the story,

Give bones to the story

So that the story tells you."

The telling of the story verifies the experience. The bones of a story need flesh, and in the retelling new and more explicit memories flood back. This is very healing for the mourners.

A problem that so-called professionals have with grieving people concerns the length of time they should keep the artefacts belonging to the deceased. Many suggest that the clothes, etc., ought to be disposed of as soon as possible after the cremation/burial. My feeling is that no one can dictate such an action. The bereaved person knows; no one else does. It is a different thing if after three or four years the place at the table is still being reserved and the clothes in the wardrobe are still on hangers; then I would have a chat with the person and see what part of active grieving has not been completed.

When my mother and father returned to their home, having spent a few days with Father's sister after the burial of their second child, all the baby's clothes and little trinkets were gone, with not even a box of talcum powder in sight. When Mother asked if there were any of her little daughter's dolls anywhere, she was met with blank embarrassment from all around. They had got rid of everything that suggested a baby or small child had ever existed. This causes such deep heartbreak for parents who need desperately to have some little trinket to comfort their vulnerable and broken hearts. Like a child needs her/his comfort blanket in times of distress, when a child dies, a parent needs the comfort blanket of their child's small playthings or, better still, their clothes with the smell of their little bodies still present.

150

I have been with parents as they held their daughter's doll between them, searching for her smell, snuggling into it to find again the presence of their little one there. In the early 1990s, I stole a baby's hospital vests and wet nappies, which were about to be incinerated after the baby's death, and gave them to the mother when she was leaving hospital without her baby in her arms. She told me years later that that was the greatest gift she could ever have received, as they did not have any clothes to remind them of the baby's smell.

Familiar smells are so comforting at a time of loss, and smells associated with a loved one bring deep comfort when all other help fails. It is primitive and when the heart is crushed and broken, we revert to our primitive natures and our senses become more aware, eg., our sense of smell and touch. Many people who suffer the depressive stage of grieving do not want to be touched. It is as if their skin becomes ultra-sensitive and the body defends itself against too much touching. I do not open my arms and hug a bereaved person tightly. I offer my two hands and, if they wish for further contact, they initiate it. I have witnessed too often grieving people being squeezed in a hug from others, even though their whole being was saying, "No, thank you, not now." Clearly, it is the sympathizer's need for this particular expression of condolence, not the bereaved person's need to receive it.

I also believe in the great healing power of photographs; so many memories come flooding back when the bereaved sit together and are visually helped to remember different scenes from the past. So much releasing of tears that still need to be shed, and the tears mingle with laughter as they remember joy-filled times amidst the sadness. If a parent dies, it is essential that the children, no matter what age, be present for such family gatherings. They must be included in all that is happening, so that they can openly grieve with the older people and realize that crying and feeling our sense of loss is natural and must not be suppressed.

I have often experienced a sense of guilt and shame in the grieving hearts of relatives of people who took their own lives. There is a sense of "I should have done something" or "I never noticed anything; s/he was a bit depressed but I thought nothing of it, they were depressed before but got out of it o.k." Always they feel they should have done something for the person who died. I help them to overcome the guilt first and then active grieving ensues. I show them how prayers and incantations are helpful for the soul of the dead person and how the bereaved can offer real help now, where help is truly needed. This is a great blessing as they can spend time assisting the soul to find light and peace instead of condemning themselves and feeling ashamed of actually asking for help. I do believe that no situation is hopeless. We can all find a way to express our love and our gratitude, our sense of sorrow and pain, without having to take on the burden of guilt and shame. There used to be a practice in the Catholic Church whereby the body of one who had committed suicide was not allowed to be buried in the graveyard but had to be laid to rest in another field away from the church. This was a most inhumane custom, one which heaped shame, guilt, and remorse on the poor relatives. The act of suicide had to be seen and judged by all as sinful and the dead person was not worthy of Church anointing or burial. Babies who had died at birth before they had time to be baptized, or who were stillborn, were also deprived of a Church burial or ceremony. Imagine the added agony for dear parents whose grief was not allowed the comforting ritual of Church burial and ceremony. Such a rule was treachery beyond belief with no mercy, understanding, or human decency. Jesus the Christ's words, "Judge not and you shall not be judged" and "Suffer the children to come to me for such is the kingdom of heaven" come to mind.

For many bereaved people living alone, the time after the cremation or burial can be a time of loneliness and intense sorrow. The friends have left, family disperses, there is no one around to talk with and the house becomes bare and unbearable for many. This is a time when a visit from a neighbour can be of wonderful healing help. Some communities form a group of "compassionate friends", comprising of people who visit the bereaved every week and help in any way they can. This is so comforting and healing and a real work of compassion. These people are doing what I call works of mercy and I honour the unconditional love with which they interact with others. Thank you. Other grieving people want to be left alone as they need time to their own thoughts and tears. All we can do is offer our loving time and let them decide if they wish to accept it or not. Great sensitivity and unobtrusiveness is essential in all our dealings with bereaved people. They need to be in control as much as possible. Their lives have been unpredictable since the death and dying of their beloved one and any semblance of normality is necessary for their healing. They must be given choices all along the way.

After some time of active grieving—and it differs for everyone, as I said before—it is important that the bereaved have a chance to actively let go also and move on to the stage of healed acceptance and reach out to the world again. They will know within themselves when the time is right to do so and, if they have been allowed to actively grieve their losses, it will take less time to reach this place. The ritual of letting go will help them to concentrate now on their own life, to uncover the joy within their souls again and plan a life for themselves without their partner, friend, or relative. One man whose wife died confided in me, "Phyllida, I don't think I will ever smile again." He did not need any comment from me. I simply took his hand in mine and held it a while. He let it go in his time. He also smiled again in his time.

The Ethics of Assisting Another
in Their Desire to Die

The Celtic people believed that we are allotted a certain number of years on earth after which time we shape-change into a new life. They believed that the veils between the worlds of seen and unseen are quite thin and at certain times, e.g., in the night-time, these veils disappear and the old ones can talk with the dead and exchange stories. The idea of pain being synonymous with bodily or earth life was an accepted truism with the old ones. However, suffering was something that the mind brought in to emphasize or draw attention to the pain. Oftentimes my Nanny would be heard saying to the dying person, "Sure, you need not be suffering at all when you believe your mother and father and old ones are waiting for you." In other words, do not give too much attention to the pain; feel it and then be in another state of awareness.

Whilst it seemed natural to be of help to another in dying without suffering from pain, the idea of actively killing them would have been unnatural. When warriors were wounded in battles, their pain was relieved by the application of particular herbs and berries and they immediately returned to the battlefield and went on with the warring. Animals and humans alike were healed from such natural potions. The safe passage of a child at birth was assured by the means of body massage and herbs. Likewise, the old medicine women administered special concoctions rich in contraceptive properties to women needing contraceptives.

When a dying person had finished her earth life to her own contentment and was waiting longer than she had desired for the last breath to take her to the Summerlands, she was helped along by the medicine women by means of certain breathing techniques and the application of specified body pressure points. We call them acupressure points. These aids were not looked upon as killing or unethical as we today suppose but were natural ways whereby the soul could be freed to live outside the body—freed from the constraints of the density of earth, before the mind could attach suffering to the process. I recall as a child how animals were given certain herbs and berries to help them die peacefully if they had been in pain after an accident. I have been taught that certain breathing techniques and pressure points applied to certain parts of the physical body help the dying leave the body in a state of peace and joy. I know that somehow the ancient yogis also knew these methods. Naturally,

I do not teach such powerful techniques to another, as one cannot intervene in such a way in another's death. Ethically, in this country it is unacceptable for many sound reasons. I also believe in the soul's own timing, which is always perfect.

It was said of Brigit that she was able to bring life to the dead by breathing on them and also to help one to die peacefully by "taking the third breath out of them and sending it to God".

PART FOUR

Being with the Bereaved

Supporting Bereaved People

You cannot be fully present to bereaved people, if you have not first grieved your own losses. This for me means that you have reached and have worked through to the sixth stage of the grieving journey. This sixth stage I have added to Elisabeth Kübler-Ross's "Stages of Letting Go", the term used when people speak of what I call "integration" . . . and that is, Reaching Out. This stage for me is very important as most of the other stages, i.e., denial, bargaining, anger, depression and acceptance, are somewhat internal and naturally more subjective and often experienced alone.

The acceptance stage is when we have integrated the grief and are aware now that what was so painful, so heart-rending has happened and we accept this as fact. But it can also be a lonely place where, whilst fact is fact and the missing the beloved still absorbs a lot of one's time, it doesn't overpower one any more.

This stage of reaching out to the community again is for me a vital passage because it helps one to become part of another dynamic, the community of other human beings around us.

When we are with grieving people the greatest gift we can possibly offer is our undivided presence. Often this presence takes the outer form of listening with an attentive heart. And of course, the heart hears the unspoken words because it understands the world of symbols. And the way we language our interactions is important. Asking skilful questions at the right time promotes a sense of ease and friendliness as opposed to giving advice and appearing to be a know-it-all!! The only one who knows the real story is the one experiencing it. We, the supporters have to listen and learn from both the dying and the bereaved.

If you are visiting someone who has just buried her mother and you want to offer empathy you might say for example:

"Ahh this must be really sad for you, Mary, I'm sorry you have to go through this loss and I know you were very close with your mother." Or you could offer, "I can only imagine what you are going through, dear Mary, such a loss. Is there any way I can support you?" Of course, it can be in practical ways like driving to do shopping, or collecting children from school. Or as I was told by some bereaved person, that the pot of soup I made every day was a wonderful help, as many bereaved people do not think of eating good, nurturing food.

Also, it is important to remember that bereaved people are usually in such emotional states of consciousness that they cannot think cognitively. I noticed this with many dear ones whose beloveds had died. They were unable to put notices in the paper about the death of their father, mother etc. The cognitive, rational mind gives way to the emotional heart and supports it to have its space.

It Is Their Story

It is important when speaking with bereaved people that you really hear their story; this is part of the healing process. They will know exactly the time the death happened, what they were doing, who said what and the time they said it. It is as if time froze for them and was encapsulated in a bubble of memory, never to dissipate. It is so easy when sharing with bereaved people to make it your own story...let me share with you how many conversations go...

"Hello, John. I heard your father died. This is so sad for your poor mother and sister. And of course for you too, John. My father left us, died I mean, when I was four years old. My mother died when I was only 17. This was very sad for us all. I was the oldest and had to care for the others like a mother and father, but aunt Brenda then lived with us. Did you know Brenda, John? She was a lovely woman. She died ten years ago etc., . . . "

Needless to say, this does not help anyone. Least of all poor John. Neither does it help to say things like e.g., "Well at least they had a good life." Or if it was a child that died to say, "Well at least you're young enough to have another child." We all mean the best and sometimes we are just a wee bit unskilfull with our conversations with the bereaved.

But I believe that healing is always happening and the dear passing time assists in that healing programme. More and more we see that love is the only constant, the only healer in the end.

"To be loved in life,

To be loved into death,

That transcends death itself

And carries the one left behind

Into that space where love cradles them both."

The Golden Breath of Love

This exercise may be used to support a friend or relative who is grieving.

Remember, dear ones, this is a practice you have to build up with yourself. You will know how many breaths are right for you in the beginning. If breathing slowly and deeply is new to you, then take it very easily and slowly.

Start with two breaths and then three slow breaths in the beginning and do not try to do any more. You will find that the practice also helps to strengthen your lung capacity for breath…Be wise and take it slowly…As always let love be your guide in all things…

the golden breath of love

Sit in a quiet place reserved for your practice; a place that holds loving energy from day to day.

Light your candle and close your eyes.

Still your inner being with a slow in and out breath.

Breathe like this for five deep breaths. Relax.

As you breathe slowly keep your attention on the here and now.

With the in-breath feel the words "I am here," as you breathe out feel the word "now".

Allow the body to rest as much as it can. If you need to move do so and then relax again into the breath.

All is well…
Now imagine that as you breathe in, this time a golden light

appears at the top of your head and as you breathe out the light comes down through your whole body systems through each individual cell into your feet.

Keep it there.

Imagine your whole being filled with the golden light.

Keep breathing slowly and keep drawing down the light through the top of your head.

(If you feel a headache then slow down as too much energy is coming in. You are in charge of all that happens.)

Now as you begin to fill up with this golden light imagine the person you are sharing this gift with.

Now "feel" them sitting in front of you smiling and happy to share from the golden light.

Begin to slow your breath again and feel the energy of the other person.

Now as you breathe out this time, direct the light to their outline.

Keep sharing and feel the light transforming the old energies into bright sparkling light of gold. This is the highest energy you can share.

See the other smiling all the time and just sharing the light that is there between you both.

After ten slow breaths begin to take the light back into yourself again.

Feel the other leaving slowly and with great gratitude in their heart for the gift you have shared with them.

Now slowly put one hand on your own *hara* (below belly button) and the other on top of your head.

You are sealing in the light.

Your intention is that whoever comes in contact with you this day will also be blessed because of your willingness to share this light.

This love. This healing. This loving energy.

When you have done this:

Relax and slowly open your eyes without moving your body.

Take in the room again.

Slowly take off your shawl.

Blow out the candle.

Breathe in three deep, slow relaxed breaths and leave the room or sacred space. Slowly.

Take some water and walk around for a while.

Open the window and breathe in the freshness of the energy from nature.

This practice when done many times fills you up with such healing energy, and know that what we do for another comes back to us, so we are only ever receiving!!!

Sacred Ritual for Bereaved People

When we do rituals for the dead, we should not repeat these rituals for more than seven days, because the departed need to go on their own journey and should not be attracted back to what they know.

Having found out the spiritual path people follow one could offer the known rituals from their tradition. It does not matter if the people are religious or not, we can offer a ritual regardless. The wording may differ here and there, but the essence remains one of integrity and honouring the dearly loved departed.

A sacred ritual to help bereaved people to somehow integrate the sense of loss and deep grief could be the following:

---

lIFE celebration

Place on your altar:

- A photo of the deceased person.
- A remembrance of them like an article of clothing such as scarf, hat, blouse. In the old days it may have been a pipe or cigarettes! Or even a box of favourite chocolates!
- Something they liked to have near them such as a book, flowers they liked.
- A white candle.
- Oil of lavender or sandalwood, placed in a small container.

Begin the ritual with welcoming everyone there. Name each person individually.

Share what the ritual is about, i.e., a celebration of the life that John or Mary lived and how through this ritual we can help each other to bring out the lovely memories and integrate the experiences we had with the beloved.

Say a few words about how you, the celebrant, knew the departed or if you did not know them.

Each person is asked to share what their relationship with the beloved was like and what they miss most about them now.

Maybe a song or a poem could be shared that reminds them of the departed.

We end the ritual with a short blessing to send everyone away with the love they all shared, supporting their journey without the beloved that has passed over.

Suggestion of heart words that might be shared:

We loved you in life dear . . . how could we forget you in death.

The closeness we all shared has not diminished but still flames in our hearts.

The moments that brought joy to our days will not fade upon the passing of time.

The love we felt can't die but will last until we say hello again.
Seá.

A few lines from a song that I wrote to a friend in the 1990s:

Love survives the darkest night
Cause love can never die.
And though the heart in sorrow mourns
Love survives goodbye.

Other Rituals Celebrating
Transitions in Life

The following rituals may be initiated by anyone with a sincere wish for the spirit of love and compassion to heal and transform. I believe that the more conscious we become, the more we will appreciate the world of symbols and ritual. If you really believe that all and everything in our world is there because we have willed it so to be, then all and everything is our teacher. We have to learn to be more attentive to the potential healing within every messenger.

Listen to your inner guide and hear from its wisdom. The right intention is all you need to be able to celebrate any transition or "big step" in life from birth to death. Ask your guides how to begin and ask Brigid to be in your heart, thus directing your every decision. In time you will be confident to initiate any ritual that is called for celebrating. I use the word "celebrate" rather than "perform", as the latter may suggest an actor versus audience relationship and this is not the correct setting. In ritual, everyone present brings the blessing and, as mentioned before, witnessing is an all-important element in ritual.

If you have an intuition that you would like to start working with ritual in your community, do not let the fear of "I am not good enough" keep you back. I encourage you to go on and begin in a small way with small rituals to begin with, and find a supportive other to assist you. This way you will help to bring back the rich and blessed customs of our ancestors in your part of the world. May love infuse your celebrations to keep the stories alive so that your children and their children may be the richer for them. *Seá.*

Birthing rite	Grounding the Divine
	Celebrating the day of conception
Naming ceremony	Being called to the family and kinsfolk
Sacred blood ceremony	At beginning of menstruation and puberty
Leaving the hearth	Leaving home

Sexuality rites of passage	First sexual encounter
Hand-fasting	Marriage
Priesting	Initated into Priest/ess
Crowning (Croning)	Wise woman
	Passing on the gifts to the family
Serving elder	Wise man
	Passing on the ways of the community
Watcher with the dying	Watching to the fifth Áite
Grieving rituals	Letting-go rituals
	Mutual agreement on separating consciously
Medicine healer	Healing with herbs and earth
Spirit caller	Calling spirits to assist
Community rituals	Celebrating the cycles of the year
	Inviting stories that want to be told

PART FIVE

Lessons from the Heart of Nature

Nature Is Our Guide

We are so deeply loved, so compassionately cared for, which means all that is holy and whole-making is happening to us at all times. We are forever being brought into balance and harmony. Our thoughts are indeed our creations and have manifested as such in the cells of our bodies.

As we are connected to our family tree not only by blood, but by the energetics of thought patterning and systemic thought conditioning we still hold trace lines in our psyches of what our individual families held as belief systems, or cultural systems of regulation. Held over a long time, these beliefs created chemical patterning in the nuclei of the cells in the body, either strengthening or weakening the immune responses.

If we want to find a model for compassion, we can go to nature. And it is all about love, compassion and harmony. Nature shows us how trees live in harmony with grasses, seas communicate fully with mountains, animals obey the changes of the seasons without judgment, the flowers in the meadows cohabit with herbs and various plants , all cooperating with the internal wisdom that governs all creation and leads to unity consciousness.

Harmony and equilibrium are ubiquitous in nature. Creation obeys the laws of the universe and by so doing creates abundance for all. Thunder roars into lightning and creates upheaval in order to bring things into balance again . . . this is an act of loving kindness. Storms rumble and heave, creating gigantic waves against the rocks on which they lash with horrific power. But the seas are neutral, they have no ill intent. They do not judge and compare. Nature moves in answer to an inner ignition, to an inner knowing.

But the inner landscape of human beings does not always enjoy this state of equilibrium and balance. Our inner worlds are often in conflict with the outer and this is due to the ways we create our worlds.

When we create from thought patterns of joy and well-being the outer reflects this. When we create from a thinking model of judgment and poverty consciousness, that is what appears on the outside. As within, so without, is a law of the universe which nature observes and honours.

We humans have not been living in peace with ourselves or with the universe. Therefore, we separate ourselves from the rest of creation and believe ourselves to be of higher intelligence and integrity. We have done this to our downfall. And this story of our undoing began long before we came to inbody this time.

The Seasons Are Our Teachers

When we look at the four seasons we see how far we as human beings have travelled from our natural inner mentors.

Winter is the first season according to the Celtic wheel of life, she is the heralder of decay and destruction, the Cailliach, transformer, Kali Shakti, the Kali Yuga, the destroyer, the shape-changer of all created phenomena. She who turns us inside out and outside in to teach us how to truly live with and in the soulful nature of paradox, where all will be stirred in the huge Cauldron of Brigit, and all that is not pure love gets fired in the sacred alchemy of love.

> First we have to die…Winter
> So we can blossom…Spring
> Into maturity…Summer
> Then we transform…Autumn

Spring is the time for young Persephone to jump into life with abandonment and joy. We know this place in us and for some of us it will have been a long time ago! But she still dances in our older bones. The traces of her dance are often seen in older people when they are with young people! Traces of a much younger energy, smiles on their faces and they cannot conceal that vital memory of energetic movement and flexibility. It reminds them of first love that transformed their lives completely with its irrational joy and pain wrapped in one heartbeat. Spring is the natural time of budding and new green growth.

Summer is that wondrous bursting forth of the sap of soulfulness in all her nurturing energy.

I recall years ago when Summer came and the sun dared to touch the tip of the Donegal hills, my heart used to cry in sheer delight. As a child I was never allowed outside during the foggy and rainy days because I was "delicate", meaning my lungs were not able to breathe in such dampness. (This was not the only reason of course that I had delicate lungs. That was the outer environment that contributed to this condition.) Being indoors of course was just as harmful because we lived in a big house which was damp and dark and not much colour in those days, 70 years ago, to cheer the hearts.

But I did see the sun in summer, shining half-way down the hills, stopping short at the ridge of the Atlantic, which was too fierce for the sun to penetrate. When it got warm I was allowed to go outside and play. Such a joy for the child in me! I still feel this inner delight when the sun shines, a kind of welcome to me at last to take part in the external world of people and noises and yes, delight!

Of course, Summer is about blossoming into life, colours floating in the very air we breathe, fullness of form taking shape gradually, green, and yellow and purple and red, ahh the wonder and the magic of it all! I bless the nurturing of Summer, the mother, the red blood of passion in young men, the hormones slightly settling after springing into the blood, the hope of child-carrying for women, the excitement of creating our own dream of a definite, (we think!) future, the harvesting of our passions.

The welcoming colours and hues of Autumn somehow help us to realize that Summer is past and the shedding time is nigh. Not only in external nature around us but also within our human nature. That time when we realize that the years are passing and there's still much to realize, much to engage in before winter turns everything around again. Ahh, how nature knows her inner timing. This, I believe, is something we have almost lost.

There is a time to speak, a time to be quiet, a time to break down, a time to build up, a time to say yes, a time to say no, a time for outer journeying, a time for inner journeying, a time for love, a time to feel fear etc. (I am paraphrasing from the Book of Ecclesiastes.) When we truly have reached our natural inner authority, we will not have to depend on others to dictate to us our timing of things…we will know the changes within, we will be led by our inner tutor, the intuition. Nature depends on instinct to guide her transformations, we have intuition. Let us listen deeply and hear the voice of wisdom.

Winter, the Season and Bringer of Mercy

The wisdom and compassion held in the season of Winter is shown in its openness to death and dying. This openness is in its willingness to allow all that is alive and vital to be cradled back into the rich, dark wombing of the earth again, there to remain, in the silent presence of clay nurturing until the first movement in the Dance of Renewal comes around again. The enthusiastic, youthful form of the beautiful Persephone raises her toes above the clay altar and seduces colour, fullness, definition of forms to enliven the earth. And all the while the ancient mother Birch, like Demeter, the mother of youthful Persephone, and grandfather Oak look on, with a knowing tender smile, glad at the return of vitality.

Although fully poised for renewal of herself, Spring still hovers expectantly somewhat in places where the damp moist undergrowth of Winter feels reluctant to birth these impatient seedlings into blossoms and magnificence . . .

the timing is important and earth knows this well. I believe old, wise woman Winter often sighs for the too vivacious, exuberance of Spring like a young one undoing itself from the mother's keeping, longing for self-expression. I imagine Winter's sighs to be like my own when my children, at first delighting in my warm holding where they can sleep safely in my still presence, move to free themselves from the same arms . . . only to return later, glad of the offer of safety and safeness.

And so, Winter in her self-compassion allows these deaths, these comings and goings within herself, offering spaces for the other seasons to be expressed from her ever-present watchfulness.

Winter knows that the golden leaves of Autumn will transform because of her breath on them and then in time once more turn green when this youthful presence of Persephone seduces nature again. This is the wisdom of Winter, to allow death and transformation to be an integral, natural part of life. Does not the leaf, decomposing in Winter's earth-home surrender to this wisdom knowing that resurrection comes round again and again? Is the tree not already in the leaf? But this grand being cannot be born if the golden-brown leaf does not undergo this Alchemy of Love. So it is with us. We have to die back into the earth, wait in presence until our time is ripe for taking form again.

Ahh Winter,

Strip me naked as a leaf

So that I might dance

In the silent potential

Of what I am.

Again and again

in different disguises

Until I at last,

Exhausted from shaping myself to earth,

Tired from too many Springs

Move back into the mystery.

Honour this season of *Negredo*, you will be glad you did when Spring comes around again. And it is possible that for many, Winter will be the last visitor seasonally speaking…Spring will be for another earthing.

Move into your seasons as nature does,

No judgments of one over the other.

Does Spring complain when Summer

shows the fruits that she, Spring, had planted?

Do the leaves complain when Autumn blows the green from their
faces and abandons them to the fall?

Does Winter scold the sky because of too much rain?

If nature be our guide then let us

Welcome the seasons within our fleshed-out soul

And simply don the various garments

she presents to us

and wear them well.

When we can do this, replacing one season with another within ourselves, the
last season will simply be dropping a coat that no longer fits us. *Seá*.

connect with the ancestors

Sit or lie at ease. Imagine a tall oak tree. Feel the bark, smell it, absorb it.

Now feel the skin on your hands, your face and neck. Look at the many crevices, knots, uneven places, just like the tree.

As precious elixir called sap flows from the roots of the tree to nourish the tree, so sap flows from your dead ancestors to nourish your life.

Close your eyes for a moment. Give thanks to your ancestors and include the tree as ancestor.

Have a good look at the gnarled roots of the old tree. They are cradled in the earth living alongside millions of various living beings who find a safe homing in the all-embracing welcome of grandfather oak. Here there is no judgment, no discrimination. Here all little beings are free to make their homes.

You can also name all that abundantly nourishes you from your own ancestral roots. Name the gifts they have passed on to you. Give thanks and feel the flow between you.

Then imagine the compassion of Winter that strips the oak tree of leaves, ready to be absorbed into earth again. Their time has come.

As the leaves fall to earth, so do we. Our time will come as it has come so many times before when the compassionate arms of death will cradle us. And gather us in, so we may rest in her safe arms in peace. Ahhh, blessed rest!

PART SIX

Stories from the Heart of Death

"Do This for Each Other Often — Don't Wait until You Die"

This is the story of a warrior woman called Sarah (not her real name), a true Celt full of passion and fire which stayed with her until she died. I like to think she is still doing her own thing in her world of spirit. She had done some externalizing therapy with me and was beginning to take charge of her life. When told she had advanced cancer of the colon, she opted for placing herself in the capable arms of a group of carers called Alanna Group in Findhorn. This group of women cared for the terminally ill and dying. Sarah moved into a most beautiful old house near the beach and the compassionate group of women cared for her there until she died about two months later. These women believe that the whole person must be cared for in life and in death, so Sarah received physical, emotional, spiritual, and good medical care from them all. The doctors kept a watchful eye on medication whilst her two children cared for and loved her. Sarah did not want to be spared any of the emotional pain around her demise. There was no need to pretend at any time.

I had not been in the country and so connected with her by mobile phone and, when she got scared or insecure, she phoned from her bed and we shared all that was happening for her. Some days we spoke for hours as I listened to her fears and deep anger at how her life was deteriorating. The women who had done such amazing work, negotiating her medication and looking after her, realized that Sarah's anger and annoyances were part of her frustration with life and not about their so-called inadequate care. I was always happy to reassure them of this fact, especially after a difficult day when Sarah judged everything they did as inefficient.

The greeting she gave me on my return was, "Now I can die, I suppose," as if the angel of death herself had walked through the door!

She was determined that she would die as true to herself as possible and she certainly did.

I recall one night I said goodnight to her and drove the four miles to the place I was staying. I left instructions with the night watcher to phone me only if Sarah's condition had changed. I was happy to get to bed and get a good night's sleep. At 5 a.m. my phone rang and the watcher said that Sarah had asked to see me. I thought she was anxious and naturally drove to her immediately. When I went into her room, she looked up from underneath the blankets and the following conversation took place:

"Sarah, this is Phyllida; you asked to see me—what do you need?"
"Phyllida, I was thinking this Friday night would be the best for my farewell party; what do you think?"

"Sarah, did you get me out of my bed to tell me that?"

"Well, I wanted to get your opinion."

"Are you telling me that I had to come over just for that?"

"I am sorry, Phyllida, but I didn't think. Are you annoyed?"

"Yes, I am, and I am tired."

"Why don't you sit down here by my bed and you can talk about it?" (She was going to counsel me!)

I got a cup of tea and she talked about the gift of honesty and how she dreaded the "tyranny of niceness". She then started to talk about the party, but I was not in the mood.

"I would rather wait until your daughter comes in later and we will all talk then, O.K.?"

She was not impressed, but she saw that I was not going to go ahead and pretend I was interested, when I was just too tired to think. We had a hug and I went for a rest.

At the party, Sally, a beautiful creative dancer, poet, and singer, danced for Sarah. What an amazing gift, dancing for the dying. As Sarah loved dancing, I thought it would be wonderful to have her life danced back to her. Sally moved to the music that Sarah loved, which was John Denver singing *Sweet Surrender*, whilst the rest of us sat around, filled to the brim with appreciation of this young woman's healthy and sensuous body, spinning life and death together in a great dance. Sarah and her daughter Rose then sang the song together. Her son Jim sat on the bed with his mother, smiling that smile of "Ahh!" as they exchanged a hug. Such mixed emotions of joy, pain, grief and fierce tenderness filled the room. We were all together singing and dancing life and death. Something beautiful was born that night, something that will never leave.

"Ah, Life! Ah, Death! Ah, So!"

The week before Sarah died, she said, "Phyllida, how I would love to be able to go to the beach (directly below her window) and lie in your arms on the sand with the wind on my face."

The next day, Jim and a male friend of mine carried Sarah in a chair down two flights of stairs to the beach below and laid her on the grass. The sun was shining gloriously even though it was only April and, as we lay there cheek to cheek, Sarah told me of her deep love for nature and how she longed for the smell of the earth in her nostrils again. Well, she had it all: sand, earth, the sea, birds flying above her, green grass tickling her toes, and she was in bliss.

"Sing me one of your songs, please," she asked, and as I sang *You Are Deeply Loved*, she sang it with me and we both let out a loud *"Sea"* at the end. Life and death and sky and sea applauded. I took a tray full of earth and sand, shells and seaweed, and put it all in the bed with Sarah so that she could close her eyes anytime and be back in the earth again. It was such sweet joy to watch her close her eyes, put her head beside the tray and, with a sweet smile on her face, smell the earth smells that she loved in life and in transition.

A few days before she died, four or five of us women and her daughter took her to the bathroom in a hammock made with bedclothes and, at her request, we bathed her small fragile body. We had candles lit and some of us sang to her as others massaged her body with oils and washed her hair. She lay back in the bath and truly enjoyed the tender care and attention of all of us women. Tears filled her eyes as she touched us lovingly and said, "Do this for each other often and don't wait until you are dying, dear women." Some of us have remembered this.

On the day Sarah died, Jim and Rose spent time alone with her, speaking words of loving comfort and letting her know how much they loved her. When I had asked Sarah what she needed to hear as she began to move consciously into the next stage of her life, she said she wanted me to keep repeating the words:

"Go to Jesus; just take your foot off the ledge and see him waiting to enfold you in his arms."

She was scared she might want to hold on to the edge of the mountain and not let go into his waiting arms. As she was dying, I repeated the words over again into her left ear. Though I assured Jim that his mother was not in pain, he was anxious so he went to the chemist for some more prescribed medication. Rose was by her side. I watched by the window over from the bed in case she needed me. Rose had also learnt the words her mother had requested so she kept repeating them slowly. Then Sarah's breathing changed as I had advised it would. I still stayed by the window, encouraging Rose to be with whatever was happening, as everything was perfect.

"Go, Mum, go into the arms of Jesus. See him before you, take your foot off the ledge; you are safe."

Beautiful words of great spiritual help to her mother. I was aware of the way in which the daughter was birthing the mother into her next life of love. Then Sarah let out a long breath and died. Rose sat there quiet and peaceful. Seemingly, mother and daughter needed this time together and all was perfect. Sarah was safe; she had a smile that said "all is finished".

Fear versus Love

The two greatest emotions out of which all others are born are, I believe, fear and love. The Cauldron advises:

"Have a deep respect for fear,
for it carries within it the seeds of love."

This is a story about love, about amazing grace, that teaches the heart about fear and the grace that releases the fear (paraphrased from the hymn "Amazing Grace").

It was 1996 and I was giving a workshop in Germany. One of the participants was a man of around 36–38, who was terminally ill with cancer of the liver. His name was Werner, and he was married with a young child. He wore a rose-coloured scarf and was a beautiful singer. It was not an easy workshop, as the participants worked on the hurts and pains of childhood and externalized the anger, grief and fears associated with it. There was much crying and singing, laughing and loud sounds of healing during the four days. With help, Werner expressed his emotions, which, until then, he admitted had been lying unexplored inside him. He signed up for the follow-up workshop some months later and again wonderful insights flooded his awareness. I promised Werner that, if I possibly could, I would be with him when he was dying. I was on a personal retreat in Southern Spain in January 1997 when I got a card from a friend saying he was asking me to come, if possible. I had scheduled to go to Germany again on February 19th, to do another workshop, and I reminded Werner of this when I phoned him that evening.

"I will not be here then," he said quite clearly. I felt the urgency of his invitation.

"O.K. then, Werner," I said, "I will be with you this week if possible." I had just enough money to get me through another four weeks in Spain. When I enquired of the travel agent the price of the return ticket to Germany, he said: "798 pesetas." I realized that that was just what I had left! Naturally, I booked the flight immediately. Some things you just do not think twice about. My dear friend Helga Hermes met me at the airport and drove me directly to Werner's flat. During our conversation, she said, "By the way, there is money in this envelope that a woman left for you; she had not paid for the last workshop and you said she could pay anytime."

Well! Of course, it was a miracle for me and I was delighted.

These situations verify our business! I was in the right place at the right time for sure.

Werner and his beautiful young wife Gudrun and young child Marian gave us a big welcome.

Werner and I talked about his great fear of dying as he had been reading the *Tibetan Book of Living and Dying* and it all seemed so frightening to him. The idea of meeting demons and hungry ghosts created great fear in him. I immediately challenged him from somewhere I do not know:

"Werner, what is your belief about dying? What do you believe happens at death?"

"Well, Phyllida, I would like to think that Jesus would meet me, that love would comfort me."

"O.K., Werner, you now have a choice to make. You tell me you have only a few days to live before you die. How do you want to spend them— in *fear* or in *love*?"

"I want to spend them in love and in preparation for meeting Jesus."

"So, Werner, we will give thanks to the author of this book; I am sure it is helping many but it is not your culture or what you believe in, so you will leave it down and not read it again. We will just concentrate on love."

I was surprised at my immediate, direct intervention. Sometimes I guess one has to make decisions for another, especially if they are feeling so vulnerable and insecure.

He was so relieved to hear this and tears filled his eyes as we sat together on the sofa and began to look at his fears and see where they came from. He had a need to do everything "by the book"; after all, he was a very good lawyer with an enquiring, alert mind, who did not like to give up on anything. As he was unable to make the sound of his fears out loud, I surrogated the sound for him as he felt the emotion inside him. It was so healing for him to be able to feel the fear and then hear it echoed on the outside.

He did some drawings, as he had done at the workshop, and I facilitated his dialoguing with the pictures, which helped him deal with any unfinished business around family or friends. Gudrun was so amazing, such an intuitive, honest woman, who did not pretend that things were easy for her. Her respect for her husband demanded open dialogue and truth-telling and it was a great honour for me to be part of such healing grief. A beautiful song had come through me at the previous workshop and it became part of the deep sharing time we had together in the evenings. Each time we completed a piece of work during the day, Werner called his wife and child to his room and we all sat with our arms around each other, singing it repeatedly.

"I am with you that I might heal,

You are with me that you might heal,

We are together that we might heal,

We are healing that we might love."

On the second day, we were talking about unmet needs and dreams and he said he would love to be able to go out in the snow and feel it on his face and under his feet. The only problem was that the flat was five stories up and he could not walk down the stairs to be outside. As I looked out into the sky, I realized that there was a small balcony with a railing around it and I was excited! Werner was able to stand for a few minutes on the balcony with his hands clutching the railings. His eyes were as clear as the snow and his heart widened in him.

The rest of the day, we did more healing on his anger with people who told him he ought to be spiritual about his cancer and would not allow him to express any so-called negative feelings. How often the will of God becomes the escape route for so many so-called spiritual teachers. (I remembered the case of my own dear parents.) Instead of helping people through the stages of grief and pain and by so doing reach a place of acceptance naturally, they impose their rigid beliefs, in which the hurting human being is not considered. I reminded Werner of the time Jesus himself was dying and he asked that the chalice or Cauldron of His Agony be taken from him. He had to rebel before he could reach acceptance. He also needed his friends to "watch" with him as he went deeper into his feelings of grief, fear and tears of loss and abandonment. He needed the human presence of his friends around him.

At Gudrun's request, I explained to their son about the chrysalis pupa and the butterfly and how the butterfly is hidden inside and emerges at transformation of the chrysalis. Gudrun translated sentence for sentence and he was happy with the idea of Daddy being compared to a beautiful butterfly soaring high without pain into a new life.

Later, Gudrun shared her feelings about her husband's dying and how this had affected her relationship with him, how at times she felt angry and frustrated but had nowhere to go with it all. That evening I facilitated her to work on some of the grief which took on the form of anger and she looked much lighter in her being. It was refreshing to be a part of such conscious relating in living and in dying. These two beautiful people were not prepared to hide their shadows, no matter what.

That night, as I left the room, Werner asked me what he would do if the fears came back during the night.

"I will put this chair close by your bed, Werner, with your rose scarf draped around it." I consoled, "Jesus will sit here until I see you in the morning. If you feel any fear, reach out your hand; his hand will hold yours until you go to sleep."

Again, the answer came very directly without thought. I left knowing that all was well.

The next day, at their request, I did healing work with Werner and his wife around the issue of separating consciously from their marriage vows, which entailed taking off the wedding rings, thereby releasing each other from their vows. Before this could happen, it was necessary first to share together the joys of their first date and how they felt about each other.

I have realized through my Celtic roots how verifying and important our stories are. I have also come to realize how people love to tell of how they first met and who said what and where it happened, etc. This was so sacred to witness. Time stood still in the five days I was with this wonderful family. We were doing a lot of good healing work without having to rush anything or try to make things happen. Death had opened our hearts and we were opening our own. We were safe.

Later in the afternoon, I played Werner's guitar and sang some songs with my back to him and his wife, as they held each other and shared intimate time together. Naturally, I suggested that I would leave the room, but they wanted me to keep singing and be a container for these, their last intimate minutes. When they released each other, they said, "How amazing; the songs you sang were exactly the ones we used to love when we first met!" These included *Bridge Over Troubled Waters* (Simon & Garfunkel).

The Cauldron teaches that when two or more people share a space of unconditional love together, the Beloved dances between them. That evening, Werner and Gudrun requested that I ask Brigid for a Celtic name for their son, as they wanted him to be re-named before his father died. This I did with great joy and the altar was made; candles and oak leaves, stones and other gifts of nature adorned a small table beside the huge Christmas tree. In the ritual, the father gets to call the name first after it comes through me. How marvellous that Werner could hold his young son on his knees, bless his life, and say goodbye at the same time. In our Celtic tradition it is all-important that the son gets the father's blessing. It teaches that:

"An mac a bhfuil beannacht a Athair aige, is e solas a dhorcas fein."

["The son that has his father's blessing, he is light to his own darkness."]

My heart is opened by being with the dying and their families, so much so that at times I am astonished at the way things just come together in the way Brigid pronounced:

"When you walk your soul walk,

Your feet become light,

Your breath deepens,

Grace sings in you

And you swim in its timeless streams."

When I asked Werner the next morning if there was any further unfinished business he needed to look at, he smiled at me with such joy. Whilst he was glowing with love, however, this proved to be a difficult day for his wife, as Werner said he felt so good, as if he could get better. I understood her concern very well. She had cared for and looked after her husband with such attention and he seemed happy to let everything go and die happily. Her exhaustion was evident as we all sat and shared together. I assured her that many dying people suddenly get a remission from the illness and appear as if they will get better. It is about the healing the soul has experienced, the state of being in one's true nature, which is love. Werner was truly in love; his earth-mind had been absorbed into his soul and all that was left was pure joy. The poor body, however, was not now able to recover as the cancer had taken hold. It was time for the soul to leave.

This can be a very uncomfortable place for the relatives and friends who are prepared for the death of their loved one and have released all ideas of their getting better. I was very humbled by such truthful and open sharing as I sat between them and they cried together. We finished that session singing the words of the healing song again: "I am with you that I might heal . . ." Werner looked radiant. My feelings were that the end was very near. I was right.

He felt so good that he actually came to the kitchen when he smelt the pizzas on the grill and asked for a bite! You can imagine the shock their friend got, when he walked into the kitchen on his own, unaided by either a stick or another's arm! He laughed and we joked about his looking for pizzas and his dying. What utter naturalness and homeliness. Death is the grand destroyer of masks, we dare not wear them in her company, and she will find ways of tearing them off us.

That evening we discussed the funeral and Werner's final requests. Gudrun was determined that she would see to all the necessary practical undertakings herself and would not engage the funeral company for any of the sacred rituals. Werner's body was going to be left alone for as long as possible before touching it after he died, so that his soul could leave without any disturbance.

When I came to see them the morning of my fifth day there, Gudrun came to the stairs and anxiously said, "Phyllida, he is asking all morning for you; come."

What a sight met my eyes. Werner was well on his way, on his big adventure of dying. A sense of joy flooded the room. He was pale and tired-looking but serene. Gudrun was lying on the bed to his right side with her left arm around him and her face close to him. He was still totally conscious and bade me come closer. As he had been getting sufficient pain relief he was not suffering at all. I felt the natural thing for me to do was to cradle them both in my arms. Werner's head on my left shoulder with his left hand in Gudrun's hand and her long brown hair, wet with her tears, around him and her beautiful face smiling on him lovingly, telling him how much she loved him and that he was free to go. I usually do not go near the body but in this case, somehow the thing to do was to hold him and his wife, again be a container for their love. He was totally conscious, beautiful, and so peaceful. I softly whispered to him:

"Werner, Jesus is coming to meet you now so no need to delay,

Let the breath come and go slowly.

No need to be afraid.

All is perfect:

There's only love now; go towards love.

See Jesus coming.

No need to keep breathing in this world

Just relax completely.

All is well.

Love calls you home.

Only love now, nothing else.

You are innocent.

Follow the voice of love now:

Keep looking towards the light of love now, Werner:

Jesus comes.

We leave you with Him."

185

Within a few minutes, he looked up at me, breathed out, and then he passed away from this life form. I smiled at Gudrun and said, "All is well, Gudrun, Werner is no longer with us."

I took a note of the time, 11 am. I believe the sun shone outside on that cold day in January in Nürnberg. The sun was certainly shining inside.

We just stayed where we were, not moving for more than half an hour, then we slowly moved away from the bed. The candles were still lit. Later on little Beólan (as he was now called) came to the room, looked at his father in the bed and went out to play again. It was as if the child knew Daddy was no longer there. The butterfly had flown to the sun. Beólan had done his grieving with his father, so there was no more to do. Werner left completely without looking back. Such a clear and total de-cathexis was sacred to witness, no hanging around later and no clinging to his family. The goodbyes had been said and . . . it was finished.

Later on that evening, I showed Gudrun how to wash the body with as little intrusion as possible and how to dispose of the water and his old clothes. The Celtic Christians buried this water under a tree, thus returning the old life to the roots of the tree of life and would have burned the clothes he wore during his dying process. New clothes signified new life. My grandmother would have said, "Sure doesn't he need new clothes for where he's going?"

Later on, the rings were buried in the earth with a little ritual of giving thanks for all they had shared. They had let go consciously of the sexual energy that attached them to their relationship, thus allowing Gudrun freedom to be in another relationship if she wanted. It also made sure that Werner would not go through any lower energy states as he journeyed to the centre of himself.

I was not present for the funeral, as I had to get my flight to Spain. It was not important. I did what I came to do and that was to help Werner make a choice for love. When I returned to see Gudrun some months later, she took me to the graveyard to show me Werner's tombstone. On it were all the words of the healing song, "I am with you that I may heal."

Thank you, Werner; I was healed so much from being with you and your family.

APPENDIX

The Alchemy of Love

What sustains the universe
And all that moves
In and through it,
All that births and deaths itself
In its wild expansive creativity
Cannot be named
Other than to name it love.

And my friend
The love that separates
And wields power
The love that judges
And discriminates
The love even
That shows preference
Is no less love
Longing to grow into itself.

And that love
That balances
Centuries of grief in hours
Generations of wounding
In moments
Eons of suffering in breaths,
Is also a true face of love.

That love

That scrapes and burns

And tears the heart

From its soft nesting

And cradles it back to grace

Undiminished

Innocent

Stretched

Into the fullness of itself

That is love at last

Grown into itself.

Can you stretch your imagination with me to consider for one moment that every experience we have ever had in all incarnations were truly a search for love?

Can you imagine that all your thoughts and actions were part of this search? You did not know it at that time but you did all you could have done at any given time to find this love. Even the times when you hated yourself, when you hurt another, when you lied and were full of rage, you were searching for love.

You searched for the cultural, religious, psychological, romantic version and definition, and felt that all you received was hurt.

'Cause no one told you that everything and all is an expression of love.

Even the hatred, the lies, the bitterness, the cruelty, the self-destruction are all part of the mighty alchemist, that shows you without emotional discharge, close up, the mirror of truth.

And that truth is …

You cannot get away from love as it is the network or sacred platform within which all creation experiences itself. You learnt to call it by different names such as pain, hurt, suffering, hatred, jealousy, fear, destruction, indifference, depression and disease.

You didn't know that love is everything, therefore it is the antithesis of everything. So we have to learn to live with paradox.

When we can live with paradox and see more and more the mighty alchemist at work, we will truly have our inner eyes and ears opened into the mystery of creation and we will live with less fear of a future and see how all is forever being stirred into love in each breath until and beyond death.

Wherever there are creative phenomena, you will find alchemical interaction. It is the modus operandi of the life force itself, that transformative power in which all creation lives moves and has its being.

Chemistry is truly the handiwork of an unimaginable, intelligent and creative energy that designed it so that from one unit of matter, new and more complex substances can evolve. It is matter building on matter to produce a profusion of creations. And we are still evolving as divine beings on the earth.

Each snow crystal is a work of art, an embodiment of a supremely logical yet mysterious structure underlying all things. A new born baby embodies the vulnerability and magnificence of this exquisite life energy.

As Scottish prophet and environmentalist John Muir said:

"We are constantly reminded of the infinite lavishness of nature, no particle of her material is wasted or worn out. It is eternally flowering from use to use, beauty to yet higher beauty."

When we preface the word chemistry with "al", we get a deeper and more meaningful appreciation of the word because "al" means the Divine as in:

Alleluia Aluhem Altruism Almighty Always
Alpha Aloha Alannu Alanna Allah

This great divine alchemist stirs us all in the Cauldron of Love, transforming the prime matter of our fear-based human love into pure unconditional universal love. Spiritual alchemy is all about the transformation of the base matter of confusion and fear into harmony and balance. It is about transforming the human heart into the heart of the universe.

The greatest alchemy is love. Pure divine love transforms all in its mighty stirring of the Cauldron of Life. It also imbues the gross elements of our personalities with nothing less than itself for that which can endure the transforming becomes absorbed into love.

"We have to be born again from the flames of love's compassion," taught Brigid of Ireland. Once we surrender our physical heart to this true alchemy our hearts are never the same again, for we begin to view ourselves and the world with different eyes, the eyes of love. Scientists like Gregg Braden, Stephanie Mines, Bruce Lipton and Louise B. Young tell us that when we love, the chemistry in our physicality changes; light photons are distributed to the nucleus of the cells and we are imbued with more life force energy which in turn affects our feelings. As more oxytocin, dopamine and serotonin (hormones) are emitted into the bloodstream we experience more of the joy of life.

As the alchemy of pure love embraces our earth-minds with compassion and we begin to love from the source itself one realizes that the word "forgiveness" loses its meaning. What has experienced the hurt in us, i.e., our dear earth-minds, is no longer present, because now one is more soulfully led than earth-mind driven. When earth-mind has been absorbed into love, it cannot be hurt nor can it hurt another. Blame and guilt shape-change into compassion and empathy.

To live thus is to live peace.

To live thus is to live joy.

To live thus is to live love.

And to die in this state is to live forever.

(Maybe that is what the great alchemist Jesus the Christ meant when he said, "For death will be no more, you will live eternal life," and so it is.)

But in the meantime, we are going through what the old ones call the Kali Yuga, or what Brigid called, "the chaotic flaming fires of love, so that our love may be purified" and we do not like it, and it is not personal. There is a global alchemy at work in these times and it is not only necessary, it is timely too. And it is not a punishment or a judgment, it is natural. Our dear earth-minds are on a spiritual evolutionary journey into love and it rebels because we will never be the same again.

The ancient alchemists like Plato, Paracelsus, Cleopatra and Astra were able to transform dross matter, like sulphur and mercury, into gold or silver. Women alchemists such as Hildegard von Bingen, Maria the Jewess, Brigid of Ireland, Julian of Norwich, Miriam the Prophetess, Mary the Magdalene, used plants and nature to help heal the dross of disease in bodies. The chemistry in one being absorbed by the other, true interdependent healing relationship.

Later still alchemists like C. G. Jung, Rumi and Goethe had to undergo the cleansing fires of transformation before they could help another to look at the dross of conditioned love that prevented people from opening their hearts both to themselves and to all beings.

Brigid of Ireland said:

"When you have been
Asked back into the flames of pure love,
You are a new incarnation.
Earth-mind awareness alone
Would never kneel for this.
The longing of your soul carries you here."

The ancient Hopi alchemists taught, "Should you shield the canyons from the windstorms, you'll never see the beauty of their carvings."

In these days, the true alchemist will not prevent you from the triple burning and many wonderful healers and therapists are true modern-day alchemists.

Here are some of the stages we may go through in order to be free. And we will go through these stages again and again until we can say with the Christ . . . it is finished.

The First Stage of Alchemy according to Carl G. Jung is called *Negredo*. Jung saw this process as the psychological breaking down of the conscious and unconscious hence the dark night of the Ego. Many go through a great depression and darkness at the *Negredo*-stage of transformation. If they try to change too quickly at this stage it does not work. . . The last stage of the man would be worse than the first (Gospel), as one needs to stay with the process and be guided and helped to do so. (Many people leave therapy at this stage and say it is not working!)

It is represented by a black colour, the colour of transformation, where you enter the Cauldron. Oftentimes an illness, the death of a loved one, or past wounding will bring you to this graceful purging stage. You experience the dark night of the earth-mind. You see your shadow projections and take responsibility for this. This process takes quite some time. Patience and kindness towards yourself is absolutely necessary at this stage.

As the process of alchemy continues the separating out, the individuation takes place. The *anima* and *animus* are finding their own inner identities. The female encounters her own *Animus* and the male his *Anima* and this is not always a happy greeting! They need to discover their own inner strengths apart from one another and apart from the learnt identity conditioned by parents and culture.

Individuation is important before true unity consciousness can be experienced. We have to consciously experience separation before we can fully unite. When the male experiences his true maleness and also his own inner femaleness and the female experiences her own femaleness and also maleness they can then come together to experience oneness, non-duality, divine beingness.

The Second Stage of Alchemy is called *Albedo*, represented by the white colour of innocence where opposites are first separated before integration. Where the archetypes of *anima* and *animus* show themselves individually first and then later on, in stage three, they unite in *hieros gamos*…sacred internal marriage, union of opposites, so called. When two opposites come together as healed individuations it is known as the field of innocence…or, the return of grace. Purity of intention arises from the place of innocence so that clarity can ensue.

The integration of ego and soul was thought to result from the alchemical "magnum opus" (great achievement) and in Hellenistic and Western traditions it was known as the achievement of Gnosis, the self-knowing that Socrates spoke about which was inscribed on the front piece of the temple of Delhi. "Gnosis" is Greek for knowledge, in this case, direct knowledge of the Divine.

In the Middle Ages, alchemical work like cryptic symbolism was mostly done in secret and guided by Hermetic principles related to magic, mysticism, mythology and religion. It was seen as esoteric and many alchemists were prosecuted because of the reference to spirit or God.

At the second stage of *Albedo,* the past unconscious comes to the surface and it takes time before it is integrated. Much healing is possible at this stage, with the help of a seasoned witness. Unless self-knowledge is heartfelt, it fails to guide the psyche. I believe that the words from the Christian bible, "Be still and know that I am God", have to do with this Gnosis. It seems that when we become still, in the presence of our own soul, the knowledge of our own divinity is revealed to us. Stillness is not about being static, rather it is that mysterious depth of the unfathomable within. It is that void in which creation expresses Life or Love. The spaciousness where soul finds expression in form. In a world so full of distraction it is not easy for us to steal away and be alone with the breath of life. Silence is the womb wherein stillness is birthed, wherein God Itself flows into time and space.

The Third Stage of Alchemy is called *Rubedo*, represented by the red colour of life force, blood, integration where the union has happened; the passion of pure love fills the cells of the body and new life ensues from the fusion or unity consciousness. The third being is birthed, the holy spirit or "grace"— it is at this stage that we claim our divine nature and live from source. This stage can take centuries to reach, each incarnation hopefully deepening our awareness until we become fully conscious, fully alive.

This stage of *Rubedo* is when the white stone is added and exultation takes place. In alchemical language the internal marriage is achieved. The white queen has merged with the red king and out of their union a third being is to be birthed, that of the Golden Elixir of Life itself. The non-gendered, holy soul self. Here harmony and balance are perfected in IT. Another word for IT is LOVE, the highest frequency of all.

I have written that total integration is possible only when the opposite sides of our personality have come together and have fully integrated. Self-knowledge together with self-compassion and non-judgment bring us deeper and closer to our human divinity. And this integration is the finished work of alchemy. Out of this integration all our actions will be full of integrity and conscious awareness.

I have said also that this entire sacred unity consciousness process can take us many centuries to fulfil. The more we live fully and with more awareness, the sooner we will experience what St Teresa of Ávila and John of the Cross called the Mystical Union, the re-uniting of creator and created. But in soul language there is no time. And some of us have made the sacred contract before birth this time, to have the courage to be made whole again in the fires of life/love.

Let the alchemy of love heal our conditioned selves...*Seá*.

Naturally we can take lifetimes to reach freedom and there is no judgment. But if we truly want more freedom to live love we can choose to do so whilst still on earth. Because our lives will be more joyful and more integrated. What a way to live!!

The sacred chemistry or sacred biology of life and death is with us all the time. What has not been transformed during earth life will come up at death for recognition, so here and now is the place to create change. The Cauldron has been heating up in our private and collective lives this past 20 years or more. We are being called individually and then collectively one by one to change our belief systems and come out of old, worn-out ideologies that no longer serve us as spiritually evolving human divinities. Are you the one in your community who has signed up for this?

We cannot hold anything or anyone too tightly. This is not easy for us very human beings. Yet, the joy that lives deep under the dross of our clinging to people, places and things cannot be experienced if we try to possess them. The lesson of holding all lightly is what is being learnt at this time of alchemical changes.

Some of the signs that alchemical changes are taking place in our lives:

- We are daily full of gratitude for life and all that it brings.
- We hold no one outside our hearts. There are no judgements.
- Our shadows have been integrated and we project only love.
- We rejoice at another's success, encouraging one another to live divinely.
- No matter what appears on the outside, inside we are full of joy.
- Our language and state of mind is love; it colours our choices.
- We realize that we are each responsible for the evolution of consciousness in the world.

We are all subject to the sacred laws of creation and for too long we have not been in alignment with them. And this is the way of earth creatures. Nature will always look for balance. When we integrate these laws, we are known as helpers in the great work of transforming fear into love. And this is the greatest alchemy of all. For this we come to earth each time.

My projection is that at death, I will be absorbed into pure love and by then, the "I" of me will be transformed into pure joy. I will become the philosopher's stone, I will become the pearl of great price, I will at last be the Grail and drink for all eternity that Golden Elixir called Love. And then I will come again and again and offer the chalice to others, still in the Cauldron of Mercy willing to be burnt in the fires of love's healing grace.

But I want to drink from it now, today, before I die, I want to experience transformed love so that I may live only love in each moment. Here and now and for all time…Seá.

Love

Love as defined by Western Christianity, which has affected us all whether we be Christian or not, entails a sacrificial offering of oneself for another. We have learnt that God sent his only son to rescue humanity from the consequences of their sin, so that God might be appeased. That according to Christian doctrine is the highest offering. The message one receives from such a dogma is that to love another as God loved us is to offer ourselves for another. That is translated into living for the other, caretaking, (as opposed to care-giving), rescuing the other, trying to fulfil their needs rather than our own.

This definition of love with which our parents and grandparents lived was all about self-sacrifice and taking on the sorrows of another as our own. It was the love that proclaimed . . . because I love you, I will do anything for you, even to the detriment of my own life. There were no good boundaries. One kept saying yes to the beloved whatever the request.

We were told that Mary, the mother of Jesus, said "yes" to God out of love, even though she could not fully understand what was being asked of her. She was the good woman. Eve, on the other hand, said "no" to the Father and is still seen as the disobedient, not good, woman.

There are naturally many, many definitions of love or what we name as love. And there is also the love between people that is truly nurturing, respectful, loving, passionate, sharing and long-lasting. If the initial resonance of chemistry in the form of hormones that bonds relationships is not present then agape-type love can be a wonderful experience. This coupling relationship does not have the passion of sexuality, rather, it can possess a deep caring for one another and a continuous support of one another's lives.

When love is reduced to sentimentality or self-sacrificing in order to be loved, when we feel we have to rescue others in their pain, carry their burden for them, never want to see them suffering, this is not love, this is caretaking so that we can be seen as worth loving. This is the ego's way of preventing us from feeling old feelings of guilt and self-judgment. It is based on tribal/cultural definitions of love and becomes a defence mechanism against feelings of inadequacy and low self-esteem.

As we with humble, grateful hearts delve into the psychological and spiritual mind-sets of our departed dear ones, let us do this with honour, with gratitude and with the deepest compassion for their choices and indeed for our own. No judgment, no blame. It is because of love's faithfulness to us that is does not interfere with or judges our choices in life. It even supports our dysfunctional belief systems that can lead to disease. Can we therefore say that love even serves our diseases?

When we decide to change these inner imaginations or thoughts, to a more congruent balanced inner patterning, chemical responses happen in the brain, and neural pathways of a different, more wholesome mandala emerges. The habit of wholesome thinking then permeates the inner world bringing more harmony and balance.

When this happens, disease is no longer the outcome of inner states of consciousness. It can no longer serve us.

But in these definitions of love, it is also important to respect boundaries and not try and rescue the beloved from the consequences of their choices but to offer loving presence as they take responsibility for their actions.

The Court of Love

There is a ritual called the Court of Love, *Cúirt An Grá*, whereby we who are still embodied offer back in love what we have carried for our ancestors, *Ofrail Naufa*.

Connections to Ancestors

An Ofrail Naufa

I see them now
The whole slow caravan of pain
Caught in restless flames
Of sorrowing regret
For all they left behind
Unmet undone
All handed down again
And again and again

And now, with widened heart
I bow before my own
For they remain un-whole
Till I in holy benediction
Offer back
What rightfully is theirs
At last, an ode to love
Betwixt the living and the dead

The love we encounter in the Court of Love is about the purest compassion that is neutral in essence and is without any form of judgment.

It is about harmony, balance and wholeness, as unity consciousness is at its core. It is a deep soul feeling rather than an emotion, and it is devotional in essence.

This love allows us to take responsibility for our choices which entails experiencing the consequences for the same choices. We are treated as adults imbued with the same inner resources with which to interact with integrity in our world. We are not seen as victims who need rescuing, rather, we are seen as divine beings capable of deep spiritual resilience and non-judgment of self or others.

The strong bond of DNA binds us as family units together in a kind of magnetic way. Whilst it has the power to attract us to each other, it may also repel us. We may have a love/hate relationship with our parents and siblings, still, the relationship is there. When I eventually see what they have to teach me, the energy within the family dynamics changes and we become a blessing to one another.

It is clear, we come to earth each time to further our spiritual evolution, and many of us seeking "at-one-ment" within ourselves have resource to sacred ritual as part of our integration. I used to teach so-called Letting-go rituals, but then I saw that this was incomplete in itself. The ideology behind it was inappropriate and the wording, which is a very important aspect of ritual, was misleading to say the least.

When we say, for example, we want to let go of our rage, bitterness, jealousy, etc., or we want to lay our burden of guilt, grief or shame down, I now believe someone else in the family will take it on and carry it, i.e., literally pick it up. The moment I realized this, the grace of The Court of Love was given to me. When I saw the incongruence of what I had thought was a sacred practice, i.e., "letting go", I changed it immediately. I am grateful for the meadows of grace available to us whenever we focus sacred attention. So, rather than let anything go I integrate it deeper into the honouring place in my soul . . . where no one else has to "mind my business" because my healing is *my* business.

If we have not dealt with our shadows before we die, we will still feel this state of fragmentation, incompleteness. And it is not so easy after death to look for the healing for the unity consciousness if parts of us are still fragmented on earth. They will then naturally find a resonance with someone in the family with similar or sympathetic traits.

For example, an alcoholic who dies without having integrated her drivenness and impetuosity will also find resonance with a relative on earth vibrating at the same dull frequency. The departed, so to say, latches on, clings on to the electromagnetic field or vibration of the one still on earth and searches for alignment within their energy field. This energetic co-dependency manifests as helplessness and self-loathing in both worlds of energetic co-existence.

As above, so below . . . So the unholy web of "stuck-ness" just continues until some deeper healing ritual can transform this unholy alliance.

My friend(!), although he does not know me physically, Carl G. Jung said: "It has always seemed to me that I had to complete or even continue things which previous ages had left undone." It seems that life seeks completion in form and form seeks completion in the continuation of life.

So, it is all about seeking completion whether in form or out of form.

And we can help both ourselves and our dead relatives to find that healing, that wholeness, that unity consciousness. What helps them to find wholeness is if we give them back their honour in the form of offering them back their responsibility for what they left on earth as "unfinished business".

About the Sacred Ritual

As the sacred words of this ritual must be guarded, it is not appropriate to enclose them here. We have a group of people initiated into this wisdom and should you have a desire to do this ritual, please contact me and I will share details. What we can share here, however, is the essence of this ritual.

Most court sessions are about dealing out some degree of punishment to the so-called perpetrator and thereby showing fairness to the so-called victim. There is usually a judge or magistrate *in situ* and often a jury sits on behalf of the community. Whilst there is mercy present, compassion is not an attribute that is deemed necessary in these sessions. Nor is it expected. For sure, the so-called perpetrator will not benefit from the court hearing and it is hoped that the judge will somehow compensate the so-called victim.

In the Court of Love it is different, of course. The following are the main differences:

1. There is no perpetrator.
2. There is no victim.
3. Both have to benefit from the outcome.
4. The jury represented by the community present at the Sacred Ritual do not have to find anyone guilty or not guilty because it is not about guilt.
5. The dead relative is made whole by being offered back her/his own responsibility so that unity consciousness may be restored.

The living relative has the chance to perform this great act of compassion for the ancestor for which they unconsciously held or carried some part . . . a lost part without which the dead relative cannot evolve spiritually. And with which she/he, the living relative, cannot be free.

Sacred words are spoken as part of this sacred ritual. Each word carries importance.

At the end of the ritual we say, "Thank you." And in Irish it is "go raibh mait agaibh mo shinsear" which actually means "let goodness be with you, my ancestors."

"In the whole of creation, whether in form or not in form, there is a pulsation of longing to be at one within oneself and with all."

—L. B. Young, *Unfinished Universe*

Unfinished business does not end with Death. We carry it with us into the next life, where we regret that those left behind should unconsciously carry it. Therefore, we need to gather up and integrate all our experiences before we die, so that we can leave the earth plane in wholeness, holiness. We are responsible for the consequences of our actions left on earth and any resonance with those still on earth has to be healed. This is about wholeness, this will be our longing in whichever dimension we find ourselves.

When we do not heal unfinished business between lives, we carry it back to the earth plane in our next incarnation in order to find experiences in which to heal. Imagine the extraordinary gift we offer a dear one who has passed over from this life and has no way of healing their unfinished business! The Court of Love offers this chance. Rather than seen as an act of judgment it is truly experienced by the dead as the most sacred of gifts. When healing occurs, because both parties are ready for wholeness in this situation, lifetimes of misery and suffering can be prevented.

Human Divinity

When human beings embrace their humanity to include their dark and golden shadows as expressions of their divine nature and death as a natural part of living, they will not only contribute to their own realization but will be as beacons of light for their ancestors and children's children to the seventh generation.

The awareness of our shadows is the beginning of integration and healing. When human beings deny their humanity (their precious privilege of incarnation) they also deny the expression of divine compassion in the earth through their individual experiences.

Overview of Exercises and Practices

Creative Exercises

Practices

Index

Acknowledgements

My heart-felt thanks to Greta Croilan Pattison for her patience and diligence as she helped get this new edition of *A Celtic Book of Dying* ready for publication. You are a real Anam Croi and I thank you. Thank you also to Mary Sharpe for proofreading the additional material and my publishing friend Sabine Weeke who has been a compassionate companion and a creative midwife urging the birth of this new edition. Finally my gratitude to Michael Hawkins, friend and editor to Findhorn Press; what a joy to revisit our friendship, Michael. My appreciations also go to Richard Crookes for his creative design of cover and pages, picking up the light of the Celtic spirit.

Go mbeidh Grá an domain leibh.

[Let the heart of love be with you all.]

About the Author

Photo by Bill Cunningham

Phyllida Anam-Áire grew up in a small village in Donegal, Ireland, born into a family traumatized by grief from losing two of her siblings. In the 1960s, she spent her formative adolescent and young adult years as a Catholic nun in Dublin. Going on to raise a family in Northern Ireland with her Protestant husband of 26 years during the "Troubles", Phyllida was no stranger to death on a daily basis.

Her work with the dying, most especially her ten years working with Elisabeth Kübler-Ross, M.D., in the U.S. and Europe, mapped out her life. Having spent the past 40 years working as a psychotherapist, a continuous theme for Phyllida's retreats and gatherings is "Living Consciously into Death".

Her deep Celtic roots provide a strong creative ground for Phyllida's music and poetry. The author of *The Last Ecstasy of Life*, she has published several books and music CDs and teaches the old Celtic Rituals and Gutha, Irish mourning sounds or mantras.

Phyllida believes that her greatest achievements are her two adult children, Anthea and Richard, and she loves being a grandmother. She lives in Edinburgh, Scotland.

You can contact Phyllida at: **seabheann@icloud.com**

Also by Phyllida Anam-Áire

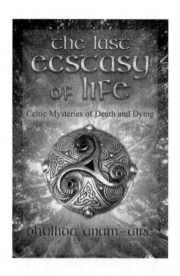

A guide to the sacred stages of the death and dying process viewed through the eyes of a Celtic Anam-Áire

Phyllida Anam-Áire provides a deep spiritual understanding of the dying process and the afterlife seen through the lens of her Celtic heritage. She offers exercises and visualizations to help prepare for death and reveals how, when the soul is fully prepared to leave its material form, the dying individual experiences spiritual ecstasy.

ISBN 9781644112656

FINDHORN PRESS

Life-Changing Books

Learn more about us and our books at
www.findhornpress.com

For information on the Findhorn Foundation:
www.findhorn.org